Young People's Science Encyclopedia

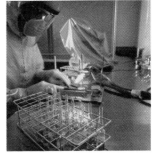

Su
Surveying
Sutherland, Earl

Sw
Swallow
Swamp
Swan
Sweat glands
Sweet gum
Sweet pea
Sweet potato
Sweeteners, diet
Swift
Swiss chard
Swordfish

Sy
Sycamore
Symbol, chemical
Synthetic fabric

Ta
Tadpole
Tamarack
Tanager
Tannin
Tantalum
Tapeworm
Tapir
Tar
Tarpon
Tarragon
Tatum, Edward
Taste
Taurus
Taxidermy

Te
Tea
Teak
Tears
Technetium
Technology
Teeth
Tektites
Telegraph

Telephone
Telescope
Television
Tellurium
Temperature
Tentacle
Terbium
Termite
Tern
Terrarium
Testis
Tetanus

Th
Thallium
Thallophytes
Thermal
Thermochemistry
Thermodynamics
Thermoelectricity
Thermometer
Thermonuclear
    reaction
Thermostat
Thistle
Thomson, Sir George
Thorax
Thorium
Thrasher
Thrombosis
Thrush
Thulium
Thunder
Thyme
Thyroid

Ti
Tick
Tidal wave
Tide
Time zones
Timothy
Tin
Tinbergen, Nikolaas
Tissue culture
Titanium
Titmouse
Titov,
    Major Gherman
Titration

To
Toad
Tobacco
Todd, Sir Alexander
Tongue
Tonsillitis
Tools
Tooth decay
Topaz
Topsoil
Tornado
Torque
Torsion
Touch
Touch-me-not
Tourmaline

Tr
Tracheophytes
Trade winds
Trailing arbutus
Train, railroad
Tranquilizer
Transformer
Transfusion
Transistor
Transpiration
Transplanting
Transplant (organ)
Transuranium
    elements
Tree of heaven
Tree-ring dating
Trench, deep-ocean
Trichina
Trilobite
Tropism
Trout
Tsunami

Tu
Tuber
Tuberculosis
Tuberose
Tulip
Tulip tree
Tumbleweed
Tumor

Tuna
Tundra
Tungsten
Turbine
Turkey
Turmeric
Turpentine
Turquoise
Turtle
Tusks

Ty
Tyndall effect
Typhoid fever
Typhoon

Ul
Ulcer
Umbra
Ungulata
Unidentified flying
    object
Universe

Ur
Uranium
Uranus
Urea
Urey, Harold
Uric acid
Urine
Ursa Major
    and Minor

Va
Vaccine
Vacuole
Vacuum
Valence
Valley
Valves, circulatory
Vanadium
Vanilla
Varicose veins
Vascular bundle

Vector

YOUNG PEOPLE'S
SCIENCE ENCYCLOPEDIA

Edited by the Staff of
NATIONAL COLLEGE OF EDUCATION, Evanston, Illinois

ASSOCIATE EDITORS

HELEN J. CHALLAND, B.E., M.A., Ph.D.
Chairman, Division of Natural Sciences
National College of Education,
Evanston, Illinois

DONALD A. BOYER, B.S., M.S., Ph.D.
Science Education Consultant, Winnetka
Public Schools, Winnetka, Illinois
Science, National College of Education

EDITORIAL CONSULTANTS
ON THE STAFF OF NATIONAL COLLEGE OF EDUCATION

Elizabeth R. Brandt, B.A., M.Ed.
Eugene B. Cantelupe, B.A., M.F.A., Ph.D.
John H. Daugherty, B.S., M.A.
Irwin K. Feinstein, B.S., M.A., Ph.D.
Mary Gallagher, A.B., M.A., Ph.D.
Beatrice S. Garber, A.B., M.S., Ph.D.
Hal S. Galbreath, B.S. Ed., M.S.
Arthur J. Hannah, B.S., M.Ed., Ed.D.

Robert R. Kidder, A.B., M.A., Ph.D.
Jean C. Kraft, B.S., M.A., Ph.D.
Elise P. Lerman, B.A., B.F.A., M.F.A.
Mary M. Lindquist, B.A., M.A., Ph.D.
Mary-Louise Neumann, A.B., B.S.L.S.
Lavon Rasco, B.A., M.A., Ph.D.
Bruce Allen Thale, B.S.Ed., M.S.Ed.
Fred R.Wilkins, Jr., B.A., M.Ed., Ph.D.

SPECIAL SUBJECT AREA CONSULTANTS

Krafft A. Ehricke, B.A.E., H.L.D.
Benjamin M. Hair, A.B., M.D.
Charles B. Johnson, B.S., M.A., M.S.
Raymond J. Johnson, B.B.A., M.Ed.

H. Kenneth Scatliff, M.D.
Eleanor S. Segal, M.D.
Paul P. Sipiera, B.A., M.S.
Ray C. Soliday, B.A., B.S., M.A. (Deceased)
Don Dwiggins, Aviation Editor

THE STAFF

Project Director   Rudolph A. Hastedt
Project Editor   M. Frances Dyra
Senior Editor   Jim Hargrove
Editorial Assistant   Janet Zelasko

Young People's
SCIENCE
Encyclopedia

Edited by the Staff of

NATIONAL COLLEGE OF EDUCATION

Evanston, Illinois

Volume 18/Su-Ve

CHILDRENS PRESS ™

CHICAGO

Photographs

Page 2: Skylab space station (NASA)

Page 3: *Top to Bottom:*
Wheatfield (U.S.D.A. Photo)
Technician capping Abbokinase (Abbott Laboratories)
Spider (Macmillan Science Company)
View of Earth (NASA)
Space Shuttle (NASA)
Bahama coral reef (Macmillan Science Company)

Cover: Design by Sandra Gelak
Sunset: Texas Panhandle (James P. Rowan)
Galapagos Tortoise (Lou Lunak)
Aloe (James P. Rowan)

Library of Congress Catalog Card Number: 67-17925

Copyright © 1993 by Childrens Press,® Inc.
Copyright © 1963, 1970 by Childrens Press, Inc.
All rights reserved. Printed in the U.S.A.
Published simultaneously in Canada.

Surveying Surveying is the science of finding the area, position, and shape of points or places on the surface of the earth. It includes the measurement of distance and angles and the figuring of elevations. The information gained is often placed on a map or chart. Surveys are made for a variety of purposes such as determining boundary lines of all kinds; finding elevation above sea level; planning for highways, bridges, and buildings; and making topographical maps.

In the United States, surveys are either public or private. Public surveys are made by national, state, or local governments. Private surveys are made for many reasons, such as the establishment of property lines and locating the position of building foundations.

In surveying small areas, the curvature of the earth is not taken into consideration. In small areas this does not cause any significant error in the measurement. However, the curvature of the earth must be taken into consideration in surveying large areas. The survey of large areas is called a *geodetic survey* and involves the use of very precise instruments to obtain accurate measurements.

Three types of measurements are usually involved in surveying—the measurement of distance, the measurement of direction, and the measurement of differences in elevation. Each requires different types of instruments.

The principles of geometry and trigonometry are applied to the readings taken from the instruments used by the surveyor. The instruments include *transits, measuring tapes* or *chains, levels,* special types of *aneroid barometers,* and accurate *compasses.*

Topographic surveying is for determining the shape of the earth's surface and locating both natural and man-made features to be shown on a map of the area. On a topographical map, surface elevations and depressions are shown by a system of *contour lines.* A contour line on a map is drawn along points that have the same elevation. Topographic maps are important in the planning of large engineering projects such as the building of highways and railroads. For such large-scale projects, *aerial* photography is often used.

H. S. G.

SEE ALSO: EARTH, GEOMETRY, MAP MAKING, MEASUREMENT, PROJECTION

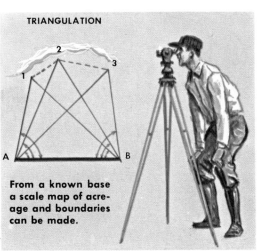

TRIANGULATION

From a known base a scale map of acreage and boundaries can be made.

Sutherland, Earl W. (1913-1974) Sutherland, a biochemist, received the 1971 NOBEL PRIZE in physiology and medicine. He discovered *cyclic AMP.*

Dr. Sutherland's research dealt specifically with the means by which hormones function. When he started his research, it was a common belief that hormones directly activate their target organs. Sutherland found that this was not the case. He showed that hormones produce an intermediate agent, cyclic AMP. Hormones control the organ's cellular level of cyclic AMP, and cyclic AMP in turn initiates or prevents cellular activity. Understanding this relationship gave new insight into a wide range of biological functions.   P.P.S.

Suspension see Colloidal state

Suspension bridge see Bridges

Suture (SOO-tchuhr) A suture is a line resulting from the union, during growth, of two parts, such as two flat bones of the skull. In surgery, it is the line formed by sewing together two pieces of separated tissue.

Swallow Swallows are common birds in the United States. They have long, strong wings and weak feet. Their large mouths and bills are well adapted to feeding on insects that they catch while flying. The largest swallow is the purple MARTIN. One of the best known is the *barn swallow* with its deeply forked tail and metallic blue-black coloring.

Courtesy Society For Visual Education, Inc.
Nesting holes of cliff swallows in steep cliffs of loess along the Mississippi River

Swallows migrate in flocks for long distances. During migration they form huge flocks at various roosting stations, different places along the migration route. The stations may be in trees, but they are more frequently in marshes. Their flight is very rapid, and they migrate only during the day.

Swallows nest as pairs and in flocks. Different swallows make different nests. They are all skillfully made in spite of the birds' weak feet and slender bills. *Cliff swallows* make nests of mud pellets; *bank swallows* tunnel into a stream or road bank.   J. C. K.

Swallowtail see Butterflies

Swammerdam, Jan (1637-1680) Jan Swammerdam was a Dutch naturalist and biologist (he would now be called a *classical microscopist*) who first described the red blood corpuscles and devised a method of injections for studying the heart and lungs. A microscopist is a scientist who studies small plant or animal structures (cells, tissues) under the lens of a microscope.

His first work, *A General History of Insects,* published in 1669, dealt with the various ways insects are transformed and their different modes of development. This work founded the science of biology. Almost all Swammerdam's work dealt with minute anatomy in relation to the life history of insects. His *Bible of Nature* is still being used by naturalists, and it contains the finest collection of observations made by means of a microscope ever published.

Born in Amsterdam on February 12, 1637, Swammerdam was the son of a wealthy apothecary and naturalist whose ships sailed to many parts of the world. The natural objects brought back were collected in his father's museum; and young Jan, who helped in the museum, studied interesting animals and plants.

In 1667 he took his medical degree at Leyden, but he neglected his practice for microscopic research. He had been introduced to a microscope as a student and had discovered the red corpuscles of the blood.

While recuperating in the country from malaria, he began to dissect and examine parts of insects under the microscope. He almost blinded himself by working in the bright summer sunlight, but he kept on working. He observed and sketched the intestines of bees and came to understand the habits of the drones and the queen. He studied the many-faceted eye of the bee. He discovered how the bee's sting worked. His most general work was his study of the process of metamorphosis in insects.

To this day, no one has surpassed Jan Swammerdam in the accuracy and fineness of his work. After his death, his friend Hermann Boerhaave collected his descriptions and illustrations of insect anatomy and published them in two volumes (1737-1738) under the title, *The Bible of Nature*. Boerhaave said of Swammerdam, "From the beginning of nature study to our own time, nobody has been able to equal his work." D. H. J.

Courtesy Society For Visual Education, Inc.

Many swamps line the coast of Georgia

Swamp A swamp is an area of water that has woody plants in it, living or dead. It may be formed when a body of water naturally takes over (succeeds) a forest. Other swamps occur when a place that has progressed in SUCCESSION to a stand of shrubs and trees becomes flooded by man, beavers, or a river.

The water in a swamp may be shallow or deep, with salt or fresh water. The soft muck bottom is rich in organic materials. A swamp is often mistaken for a bog, marsh, or fen. Swamps support a wide variety of plant and animal life—from microscopic plankton to herons, crocodiles, and deer.

The vegetation in shallow swamps

Courtesy Society For Visual Education, Inc.

Swamp waters clogged with floating plants

includes lichen, moss, liverworts, mangrove, sweet bay, alder, willow, and certain pines. Plants in the deep swamps range from orchids, ferns, bromeliads, water oak, tamarack, gum, and cypress trees.

Some swamps have been drained successfully and reclaimed for agricultural purposes. Some swamps do not have soil that is good enough to make draining worthwhile. The needless draining of swamp areas causes conservation problems. Many wild birds, small animals, reptiles, and insects make their homes or find food in swamps. Some of these wild creatures help to keep down the number of destructive and annoying insects and vermin. H.J.C.

Swan Swans are a subfamily of the family that includes DUCKS and geese. There are only eight species of swans, but they have worldwide distribution. They are large water birds, usually white, with much longer necks than geese. Their plumage is heavy and waterproof. Like some geese, they fly in V-shaped flocks. Other large, white swimming birds (white pelican, snow goose) have black wing tips.

All swans have a loud, high, trumpet-like call, but that of the almost-extinct *trumpeter swan* is the most distinct.

These birds feed from the surface and eat vegetation and small mollusks. Some feed with the head and neck underwater.

Swans mate for life. Sexes look alike and both parents care for the young. Nests are hollows in the ground, built near water. They are lined with down and made of grasses and moss. Three to five eggs are laid at a time. J. C. K.

A white American swan

F. A. Blashfield

Swarm   see Bee

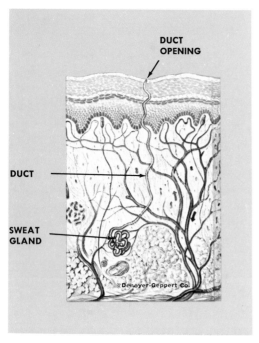

Sweat glands Sweat glands are found only in MAMMALS. Not all mammals (the ones living in water, for example) have them. The main function of sweat glands is to regulate body temperature. As sweat evaporates from the skin surface, the body is cooled. Sweat is composed of water and salts.

Sweat glands occur over the entire human body except on parts of the external reproductive structures, the eardrums, nail beds, and edges of the lips. They are most numerous on the palms of the hands and soles of the feet.

A sweat gland is a coiled tubular gland with a long duct opening on the surface of the skin through a pore.

A fluid composition of water and salt (*merocrine*) is formed continuously by cells at the base of the gland. Spindle-shaped cells around these cells contract to force the secretion into the duct.

The armpits and a few other places have very large sweat glands that produce an odoriferous secretion. This type of secretion is called *apocrine*.   J. C. K.

SEE ALSO: SKIN MODIFICATIONS

Sweet alyssum   see Alyssum

Sweet gum Sweet gum is a tree that grows in the southern United States. The shiny green leaves of this tree are maple-like, turning bright red in fall. The tree produces fragrant gum and valuable hardwood lumber.

Sweet gum is a DECIDUOUS tree. LEAVES are alternate, 5 to 8 inches (12.7 to 20.3 centimeters) long with 5 to 7 lobes that make them look like stars. Flowers form into round heads. They are unisexual, but both types are on the same tree. The fruit is in the form of spiny balls or capsules that release winged seeds. The gray bark has deep grooves. It is in the family Hamamelidaceae.   H.J.C.

Sweet pea Sweet peas are flowers that bloom in every color but yellow. The flowers grow on vines that must be attached to a support. Some stems may be 6 feet (1.8 meters) long.

A sweet pea plant must be grown in the sun in well-drained, well-fertilized soil. The seed of this annual should be sown early in the spring. These fragrant flowers need a cool temperature for they wither in very hot weather.

The leaf is made up of two narrow leaflets with climbing tendrils at the end of the leaf stem. The flowers are held erect on strong stems. The blossoms are about 1 inch (2.5 centimeters) long and 2 inches (5 centimeters) wide. To keep from injuring the plant, the flowers should be cut after they open, not plucked. The gray-brown seeds are held in a pod which is the fruit. Sweet peas are in the family Leguminosae.   H.J.C.

SEE ALSO: GARDENING, LEGUME

Sweet peas have curled and ruffled petals.

Sweet potato The sweet potato is a tropical herb grown for its large tuber-like roots. Great amounts of starch and sugar are stored in them. It has been grown as long as corn has.

There are two kinds of sweet potatoes, both in the *morning-glory family.* In one, the root is yellow, dry and mealy. The other is orange, watery and contains more sugar. The first is preferred in the northern states. Sweet potatoes are perennials but are cultivated as annuals. The trailing vines may grow to 10 feet (3 meters) long. H.J.C.

Sweet William see Pinks

Sweetbriar Sweetbriar or *eglantine,* is a rose with sweet-smelling leaves, pink flowers, and prickly stems. Though of European origin, sweet-briar now grows abundantly in thickets and on roadsides in North America.

Sweeteners, diet These are sugar substitutes (nonsugar sweet substances). They are generally used by diabetics, who must avoid sugar, and by people who need to lose weight.

Of the substances produced by science, SACCHARIN and the CYCLAMATES have been used the longest. However, their safety has been questioned; some cancer resulted in animal feeding tests.

The most recent entry into the market is *aspertame,* a chemically produced sweetener. Although it tastes much like sugar in cold foods, aspertame tends to break down in hot foods. Aspertame appears to have no ill effects; however, since it is relatively new, its long-range effects are not known.

Food biochemists continue to tests other substances. Among these are *stevioside,* named for its wild plant name, Stevia; *narangin,* a very sweet extract from citrus rinds; and *sorbitol,* a chemical produced from the berries of mountain ash trees. D.A.B.

Swelling Swelling means an increase in size. Certain solid substances such as gelatin swell in water. Swelling also refers to an enlargement of a part of the body caused by disease or injury.

SEE: PATHOLOGY

SWIFT

Swift One *ornithologist* (a person who studies birds) has described the swift as a "cigar with wings." Although it does not seem to have a tail, its very short spiny one is used to prop itself against the walls of chimneys, hollow logs, or caves. Swifts fly like bats, seeming to alternate their wings rather than moving them together.

Swifts often fly in groups, particularly when migrating. They soar, holding wings up instead of extended, and feed on insects caught in flight.

About ninety species of swifts are found throughout the world. One of the best-known species is the *chimney swift.*

Edible nests of some species are made entirely of secretions. Most swifts use a gelatinous, salivary secretion to glue together a nest of twigs. Swifts lay four or five white eggs; the young are hatched naked. J. C. K.

Swim bladder see Pisces

Swine see Pig

Swiss chard The ancient herb Swiss chard is also called *spinach beet, chard* or *leaf beet.* The leaves or tops of this plant are eaten. They are more highly developed than the roots.

Swiss chard requires a non-acid, rich soil in a cool climate where winters are mild. Seed propagation should be done early in spring. As it grows through the summer, new leaves appear in the center. The outer ones become tough and should be removed. The leaf petioles may grow 2 feet (.6 meter) long and 2 inches (5 centimeters) thick.

Swiss chard is rich in vitamins and minerals. A new variety has red petioles and gold-green leaves. H.J.C.

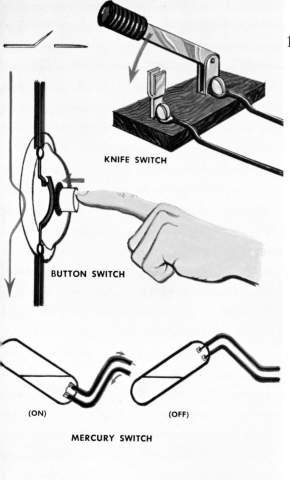

KNIFE SWITCH

BUTTON SWITCH

(ON)　(OFF)

MERCURY SWITCH

Some common types of electric switches

Switches, electric Electric switches are devices for connecting (making) and disconnecting (breaking) electric circuits. Room lights are often controlled by switches on the walls. Lamps have built-in switches. The electric toaster, mixer, stove, iron, and other electrical appliances have switches to turn them on and off.

A simple type of electric switch is the *knife switch*. This switch usually has two knife-like blades. The knife blades have insulated handles. The two blades are connected to two electric wires. The blades fit into metal slots connected to another pair of wires. When the blades are in contact with the slots, the circuit is connected or complete. Electric current then flows through the wires. The knife switch is often used as the main switch at the point where current enters a house or factory.

The *snap* or *toggle* switch is used in electrical appliances and on the walls to control lights. The current flows from one contact to the other. When the button or lever connected to the switch is pushed one way, the contacts join, allowing the current to flow. When the button or lever is pushed the other way, the current is cut off.

The door bell has a simple type of *push button switch*. When the button is pressed, a strip of brass is pushed down onto a contact point. Thus the circuit is complete.

Mercury switches are being employed more extensively as silent wall switches to control lights. A small amount of mercury is contained in a capsule. When the capsule is tipped, the mercury rolls to one end of the capsule where the two wires are located. There the current flows through the mercury and completes the circuit. When the switch is turned to "off," the mercury moves to the other end of the capsule and breaks the circuit.　P. F. D.

SEE ALSO: ELECTRICITY

Swordfish The swordfish is a long, sleek, fast-swimming fish. Its "sword," actually its upper jaw, is long and pointed, making up one-third of the fish's total length. Sometimes it is called *broadbill* because its sword is flattened, unlike the rounded bill of the MARLIN or sailfish.

The swordfish has no teeth. Its strong sword slashes back and forth through a school of smaller fish, such as mackerel or herring, until it kills enough for its meal.

Swordfish travel in pairs through tropical and temperate seas. They are a gamefish for sportsmen and harpooned by commercial fishermen for their flavorful meat. Good-size swordfish are about 400 to 500 pounds (180 to 225 kilograms). When injured, they become vicious.

Swordfish eggs look like small floating balls. Young swordfish have teeth and scales which they lose as they mature.　C.L.K.

Swordfish, caught for sport or food

Leaves and fruit balls
of the sycamore tree

Sycamore (SICK-uh-mohr) One of the easiest ways to identify the sycamore, or *plane tree,* is by the way its inner, smooth, white bark is spotted with patches of older, brown bark. The sycamore grows to be very tall, sometimes over 100 feet (30.5 meters). They grow well along river banks.

The broad leaves of the sycamore have from three to five points which are shallower than those of a maple leaf. The underside of the leaf is fuzzy. When the leaf falls, the stem has a hollow space where it fits over the smooth winter bud.

The seed-bearing balls of flowers mature into fruit balls of tightly packed seeds. They dangle on short stems on the bare tree all winter. In spring, the balls break apart into fluff that carries the seeds.

The hard wood of the sycamore makes good butchers' blocks.   C. L. K.

Symbiosis see Balance of Nature

Symbol, chemical There are 105 chemical elements known to man. Each element has its own symbol to simplify writing about it. Jakob Berzelius, a Swedish chemist, was the first to use symbols, in the early 1800s.

The simplest method for selecting symbols was to use the first letter of the name of the element, as in the case of hydrogen (H) and oxygen (O). As new elements were discovered, it became necessary to use symbols with more than one letter for elements beginning with the same letter.

Another source of symbols for the elements has been the first letter or two of their Latin names. Among these elements are: sodium (Na), from *natrium;* iron (Fe), from *ferrum;* lead (Pb), from *plumbum.*

In a chemical formula, the symbol of an element represents one atom of that element. When the presence of more than one atom is to be shown, a small number indicating the number of atoms is placed to the right of the symbol.   M. S.

SEE ALSO: CHEMISTRY, ELEMENTS, FORMULA, MENDELEEV'S PERIODIC TABLE

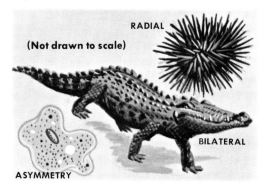

Symmetry, radial and bilateral, and asymmetry

Symmetry (SIMM-uh-tree) Symmetry is the arrangement of the parts of a living organism, either regularly around a central axis (*radial* symmetry); or placed so that right and left body halves are mirror images (*bilateral* symmetry).

SEE: ANIMALS, CLASSIFICATION OF

Symptom A symptom is a change from normal that indicates DISEASE or disorder. PAIN, swelling, and redness may be symptoms. Changes in the appearance of an organ may also be a symptom.

SEE ALSO: PATHOLOGY

Synapse see Nerve cell

Syndrome (SINN-drohm) A syndrome is a whole set of symptoms and physical signs which occur together and are characteristic of a particular disease. The syndrome, however, does not necessarily describe the disease. A syndrome can point the way to proper disease diagnosis.

Synthesis Synthesis is the combination of parts into a whole. In CHEMISTRY synthesis means the formation of compounds from elements (hydrogen and oxygen make water) or groups of elements (water and quicklime make slaked lime).

Synthetic fabric Synthetic fabrics are made of fibers that have been made chemically by man. They can be classified into four kinds depending on the process that was used in their manufacture and five sub-groups depending upon the chemicals that were used in their manufacture.

All synthetic fibers and fabrics are made of *monomers*. Monomers are active chemical compounds which, in the presence of a catalyst, join end to end either with molecules of the same compound or with different compounds to form very long molecular chains. This molecular chain is called a polymer.

There are true synthetic fabrics and man-made fabrics. In true synthetic fabrics the monomer is chemically made out of inorganic compounds. Acrylics (Orlon, Acrilan, Creslan, Veralon, Nomel, and other drip-dry fabrics) are made by extruding the synthetic polymer through a fine sieve. Polyolefins (Teflon, Butyl rubber, and neoprene) are also synthetic polymers.

Man-made fabrics are made of organic monomers. The polyester, nylon, is made of furfural found in corncobs and oat hulls. Wood and petroleum are also good sources of monomers.

Molded synthetics, the third synthetic fabric, is made by mixing the monomer and a catalyst with a solvent and then freezing the mixture. When the solvent is evaporated, a clothlike material that doesn't have to be woven results.

The newest synthetic fabrics, the eutetics, are formed by roasting a synthetic fabric such as rayon. The results are pure stretched carbon crystals called whiskers. They are used in the nose cones of rockets, heat shields, the metal skin of airplanes, and in the new F.R.P. (fabric reinforced plastic). B. A. T.

SEE ALSO: COAL TAR

Syphilis Syphilis is one of six major contagious VENEREAL DISEASES. It is caused by a type of bacterium called a spirochete *(Treponema pallidum)*.

People contract syphilis through sexual intercourse or other direct contact with a diseased person. It is detected by a blood test and can be cured by penicillin. If untreated, it can affect any part of the body, and can cause death.

Syphilis occurs in three stages. The first stage, *primary syphilis,* often goes undetected, because the symptom is a painless sore (chancre) on the genitals. Even without treatment, this sore disappears, but in six to twelve weeks the symptoms of the second stage *(secondary syphilis)* appear, which include a body rash, fever, and other signs. Again, if not treated, these symptoms disappear, but the syphilis germ will spread throughout the body, causing heart valve problems, dissolving of joints (especially the knees), brain disorders, and sometimes death (third stage or *tertiary syphilis).*

Syphilis is curable if treated with rather high doses of penicillin in the primary or secondary stages. In tertiary syphilis of over a year's duration treatment is imperative. However, even though third-stage syphilis is treated, the blood test for it can remain positive. In a case like this, the person is not contagious. Treatment does not repair any damage already done to the body.

Syphilis is again becoming widespread, because people fail to recognize the symptoms or are too embarrassed to seek treatment. Besides possible damage to the person with the disease, syphilis can be passed on to an unborn child and can result in poor bone development and brain damage. Blood tests for syphilis are required in most parts of North America before marriage. E.S.S.

Syringa (suh-RING-guh) This is the name given to several kinds of woody shrubs and small trees. They are flowering plants that drop their leaves each fall. Syringa is the genus that includes the different species of LILAC. It is also another name for the shrubs called *mock orange.*

SEE ALSO: CAPSULE, LILAC

System see Anatomy, Physiology

Systole see Heart

Tachometer A tachometer counts the number of revolutions of machinery shafts, usually in a minute. Boat and auto engines, etc., may have gauges which read in RPM.

Tadpole The tadpole is a stage in the development of frogs, salamanders, and toads. A tadpole is a gill breather like the fish. It has a tail which enables it to swim about through the water in which it lives. Sometimes the tadpole is called a "polliwog."

Some animals assume several completely different forms in their development. The tadpole represents a larval stage in the metamorphosis of a FROG. The tadpole develops from the egg looking somewhat like a small fish. After breaking free from the egg membrane, it lives for some days on yolk, and then begins to feed on algae and other small plants. During this early larval stage, it breathes by external gills which are long and branching. Later these gills disappear and internal gills are formed. Water passes from the mouth, over the gill slits, and out of a *spiracle,* or opening, on the tadpole's left side.

At first legs are not present; but later, hind legs appear, and then forelegs. The tail gradually becomes smaller, and the gills are absorbed, as lungs are formed. D. J. I. SEE ALSO: LARVA, METAMORPHOSIS, SALAMANDER, TOAD

Close-up of a tadpole
Chicago Natural History Museum

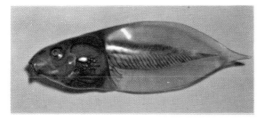

Courtesy Society For Visual Education, Inc.

First the tadpole's hind legs develop and emerge. The front legs are seen through its skin

Talc The mineral talc is a MAGNESIUM silicate. It is very soft and has a lustrous, waxlike, pearly finish. In color it is white to gray or green. When rolled between the fingers, it feels greasy. Tailors' chalk, talcum powder, and soapstone are talc products.

Tallow Tallow is a mixture of hard fats. It is extracted from the natural fat of sheep and cattle by melting the animal fat in water and skimming the tallow off the surface. It is used in margarine, soap, and candles. SEE: FAT

Tamarack (TAMM-uh-rack) Tamarack is a tree of the PINE group. Tamaracks are sometimes called American larches or hackmatacks. These trees are valuable for their timber.

Tamarack trees grow about 65 feet (19.8 meters) tall. They have the shape of a long, narrow cone. The leaves are about 1 inch (2.5 centimeters) long and are slender and blunt. They drop these leaves in the fall. They are usually found in acid soil. M.R.L.

Tamarau see Water buffalo

Tamarack tree

Scarlet tanagers have large yellow bills

Tanager Birds in this family live in the American tropics. Only four species migrate to the United States. The males are known for their brilliant feathers. An example is the *scarlet tanager*. Most tanagers have weak, tinny voices rather than musical songs.

Birds in this family are *arboreal* or tree dwellers. They feed on flowers, fruits, and insects. Tropical species are particularly fond of fruit.

Nests are made in trees about 20 feet (6.1 meters) above the ground. They are usually shallow, near the ends of branches, and made of weed stems and slender twigs. Three or four bluish, greenish-blue, or purple eggs are laid. Females hatch the eggs, but both parents feed the young.   J.C.K.

Tangerine see Citrus fruit

Tannin (TANN-inn) Tannins, or tannic acids as they are sometimes called, are substances obtained from a number of plants, such as the oak and sumac. They are used in the manufacture of leather, dyes, and ink. Tannins are soluble in water, and have a taste like lemon juice or other acid material.

SEE: ECONOMIC BOTANY, LEATHER

Tanning see Leather

Tantalum (TANN-tuh-luhm) Tantalum is a gray, rust-resistant metal. It occurs in ores with niobium. It has many uses, such as in fine electrical parts, in surgical instruments, and in special glass. It is hard and difficult to melt, but once shaped, it provides lasting products.

Tantalum is resistant to chemical action at ordinary temperatures, reacting only with corrosive hydrofluoric acid, sulfur trioxide, and strong alkalis. Tantalum is used in surgery to cover skull defects because the healing tissues grow over it easily.

Tantalum (symbol Ta) is element 73, atomic weight 180.948. Commoner compounds of this element are the chloride and the oxide.   D.A.B.

SEE ALSO: ATOM, ELEMENTS

Tapeworm Tapeworms are long, ribbon-like *parasites*. This means that they live in the bodies of other animals. They take food and shelter from their host. In return, they offer only illness.

Most tapeworms live in the bodies of *vertebrates* (animals with backbones). All adult tapeworms live in the intestines of their hosts, since food is easy to find there. Tapeworms have neither mouths nor digestive systems. Tapeworms belong to the *flatworm* group.

The life cycle of the tapeworm is complicated. In order to develop from an egg to an embryo and finally to an adult, the tapeworm must find two different hosts. Since it is not able, at any stage of its development, to move independently from place to place, it must rely upon unsanitary conditions in order to transfer eggs from one host to another.

The *beef tapeworm* displays a typical life cycle. The eggs which fall on the grass are

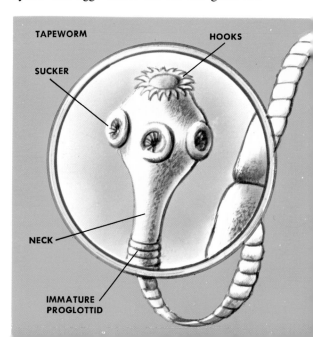

TAPEWORM   HOOKS
SUCKER
NECK
IMMATURE
PROGLOTTID

Buchsbaum

Buchsbaum

**Adult tapirs are a solid, brown-black color.
Young tapirs have stripes and spots**

eaten by the cow. In the intestine of the cow, the eggshell is digested off and the embryo is released. After boring its way through the intestinal wall, the embryo enters the blood-stream and is carried to a muscle where it remains. It develops into a sac, or *bladder,* containing a head. When man, the second host, eats uncooked beef containing the blad-der, the embryo head attaches itself to the intestinal walls and develops into an adult. The mature tapeworm produces eggs that are eliminated from the intestine with the feces or waste materials.

A tapeworm is often described as made up of sacks of reproductive organs. Since the transfer of eggs from one host to the next is so chancy, the major activity of the tapeworm is that of producing eggs. As many as 1000 a day may be produced by one adult.

The tapeworm is made up of individual sections called *proglottids.* These are joined together behind a head or *scolex.* Since new sections are budded off behind the head, the most mature sections are at the end of the body. Within each proglottid, a complete set of male and female organs develops. After the eggs are fertilized, the sex organs degenerate, the eggs mature, and the "ripe" sections de-tach from the worm and pass out with the feces.

Like most parasites, the tapeworm adapts itself to a parasitic way of life by losing or changing many of its structures. The digestive system disappears and the muscular and nerv-ous systems are reduced. The outer covering of cells secretes a thick, protective cuticle.

E. P. L.

SEE ALSO: PARASITE, PLATYHELMINTHES

Tapir (TA-purr) The tapir is a shy, hoofed mammal that lives in the thick forests of Malaya and South America. It feeds at night on fruit and leaves. Since the tapir likes to roll in mud and bathe in rivers, it lives near water.

The almost hairless and tailless tapir is about the size of a large pig. In body and head shape, it resembles the pig. Instead of a snout, it has a short trunk. Except for the Malayan tapir, which has a white back, the adult tapir is black-brown in color. The young of all species have light spots and stripes similar to those of the wild pig.

The tapir is a hoofed mammal. The four toes on each front foot and the three toes on each back foot are enclosed in individual hooves. Since the main axis of the foot passes through the largest toe, the third, the tapir is an *odd-toed* or *perissodactyl,* like the horse and rhinoceros.

Tapirs are often called *living fossils.* Fossil tapirs, which date back 70 million years, were similar to living tapirs. These animals have shown fewer evolutionary changes than have other hoofed mammals. E.P.L.

Taproot see Root

Tar Tar is a brownish-black, sticky substance obtained by DISTILLATION of organic materials such as wood, waste fats, petroleum, coal and peat. Tars have wide uses, such as for road surfacing, paints and other wood pre-servatives, and for sealing roofs.

Distilled coal and PETROLEUM give tars having an alkaline reaction, but wood tars are slightly acid.

A variety of substances made from tars include dyes, perfumes, drugs, insecticides, explosives, moth balls, a germicide (pyri-dine), carbolic acid, an artificial sweetener, pitch, film and photographic chemicals, and some plastics. D. C. H.

SEE ALSO: COAL TAR

Tarantula see Arachnida, Spiders

Tarnish see Rusting

Taro tuber and "elephant's ear" leaves

Taro (TAH-roh) Taro is a tropical food plant. Its large leaves and flower stalks are the only parts of this HERB that grow above the ground. Stems and roots are both in the soil.

The large stem or CORM produces lateral TUBERS. These are filled with starch and eaten like potatoes. The FLOWER stalk (*spadix*) is surrounded by a petal-like leaf. The fruit is a berry. *Dasheens* are taro sprouts gathered in the spring and prepared like asparagus. Taro is propagated by stems. It is in the family Araceae.   H. J. C.

Tarpon These game fish are silvery iridescent in color. They may weigh up to 300 pounds (136 kilograms) and are found in the warmer waters of the Atlantic. Their scales are large and thick. Between the jawbones under the mouth is a bony plate. Tarpons are heavy-bodied with a long filament extending from the dorsal fin.

Chicago Natural History Museum

Tarpons have several primitive features. Their fins are soft rayed like those of HERR-INGS and SMELT, and pelvic fins are on the abdomen. The air bladder connects to the throat, pelvic and pectoral girdles are not attached, and VERTEBRAE of tail and head sections are alike.   J. C. K.

Tarragon This is a small, green, perennial HERB related to *sagebrush*. The leaves of this flowering plant are used for seasoning such foods as vinegar, sauces, salads, and soups.

The leaves have a pungent flavor that comes from the essential oils produced by the plant. The oil is used in perfumes.

Tarragon is native to Western Asia. It belongs to the Compositae family.   H. J. C.
SEE ALSO: SPICE

Tarsier see Primates

Tatum, Edward L. (1909-1976) Edward Tatum, a U.S. geneticist and biochemist, shared the 1958 NOBEL PRIZE in physiology and medicine for research in the study of *Escherichia coli* bacteria and its reproductive method.

Dr. Tatum's research association with Dr. George W. Beadle in the 1930s and 1940s dealt primarily with the metabolic activity of insects. Their research examined in particular the fruitfly *(Drosophila melanogaster)*; a red bread mold *(Neurospova crassa)*; and later the chemical processes of *genes*. They studied the relationship between nutritional requirements and genetic changes, and concluded that genes act by regulating specific chemical processes in the organism. Altered or impaired genes cause hereditary changes in metabolic activity. Their work helped scientists understand the manner in which genes initiate change in the evolution of an organism.   P.P.S.

Taste Taste is one of the six senses. The areas for tasting are usually found around the mouth and nose. Most mammals have four kinds of taste sensations—*bitter, sweet, sour* or *acid,* and *salty.* Cells, mainly on the tongue, pick up the stimulus when food is dissolved. A dry object on a dry tongue has no taste.

Taste cells are found in other places in the mouth as on the soft and hard palates, epiglottis, tonsils and walls of the throat. These places, however, have very few in relation to the number on the tongue, which probably has up to 10,000 taste buds. The related areas of taste are more evident in youngsters, so that as one ages one declines in the ability to taste.

The tongue has minute projections on it called *papillae.* Embedded in the mucous membrane between these little mounds are bundles of cells which form a *taste bud*. The particular cells are long and narrow. The ends of the cells at the surface of the tongue

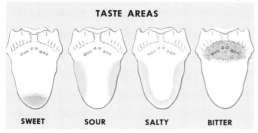

TASTE AREAS

| SWEET | SOUR | SALTY | BITTER |

Taurus, the Bull

have tiny hairs or *cilia*. They are exposed to the outside by a small opening called the *taste pore*. The other end of these elongated cells are in contact with the dendrites of neurons. The sensation is passed from the cilia through the cells to a cranial nerve which carries a stimulus to the taste center in the cerebrum. Here one interprets it as salty, sweet, bitter or sour.

The sense of taste is very closely associated with the sense of smell. That is why a person with a bad cold, whose nasal passages are blocked, cannot taste his food well.

Most vertebrates have taste areas in the mouth but some invertebrates can pick up taste stimuli over various parts of their bodies. Certain insects, for example, have front legs more useful to detecting taste than any part of the mouth.   H. J. C.

SEE ALSO: SENSE ORGANS

Taurus (TAWR-uhs) Taurus, the bull, is the second sign of the ZODIAC. It is one of the most distinctly marked of the constellations, and is readily observed in the winter months. It rises in the eastern sky, to the north of ORION and contains 145 stars. Easily recognized parts are the *Pleiades* and the *Hyades*.

The Pleiades, or Seven Sisters, form a tiny dipper-shape, so small that it is blacked out by the tip of a finger held at arm's length. Nonetheless, six of the stars can be seen with the naked eye. The Hyades lie near in the shape of an isosceles triangle, which is open at the end. It is bright and very regular in shape. Associated with it is *Aldebaran,* a reddish-colored, first magnitude star, considered the bull's eye.

In mythology, the Pleiades were the seven daughters of Atlas who were transformed into a group of stars—the seventh, or invisible one (to the naked eye), is the "lost" star hiding in shame because she loved a mortal. The Hyades were half-sisters of the Pleiades. They wept because of their brother Hyas' death, a myth which probably developed because in parts of Europe their advent, or appearance, marks the beginning of a rainy season.   D. J. A.

SEE ALSO: CONSTELLATION

Taxidermy (TAX-sih-der-mee) Taxidermy is the process or science by which animals are preserved and prepared for display or study. The methods vary for different kinds of animals. Great skill is needed, as well as knowledge of the *anatomy* or structure of the animals being prepared.

The word taxidermy means "sorting skins"; but it includes much more than sorting, arranging, and preparing the animals. It involves the setting up of natural-appearing habitats and display arrangements so that the animals appear to be in the proper surroundings. This is most important to the "real as life" look of the animal groups seen in museums today.

Taxidermy once meant stuffing dead animals. Although some of this was done to preserve trophies of the hunt, the art of taxidermy was furthered most by those interested in developing collections for commercial or educational purposes. Work in this field was done in the 19th century in France. Later, in America, advancement was made in taxidermy procedures. Professor Henry Ward set up an establishment in Rochester, New York, to supply specimens to institutions throughout the country. Today, taxidermy work is largely an activity

HOW TO STUFF AN ANIMAL

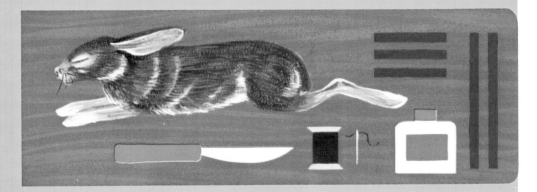

This experience is for young students of science interested in contributing to a collection for a school museum. Many vertebrates may be stuffed for a comparative study.

1   Begin with a freshly killed animal. An adult should supervise the use of chloroform.

2   Separate the fur, feathers, or other covering when cutting through the skin. When the animal is sewn back up the coat will cover the incision.

3   Skin the animal as carefully as possible. Rub borax powder into the hide on both sides and permit it to stand for several hours before removing.

4   It will be necessary to cut off the appendages and skull. Soak these in borax solution overnight.

5   Stuff the trunk with cotton. Fasten dowel rods to the appendages and insert them into the original openings. Sew up the incision in the pelt.

6   Small buttons can be painted to mimic eyes. Glue them into the sockets.

carried on by museums, universities, and the present Ward establishment.

Techniques for preparing different kinds of animals vary. *Mammals* and *birds* are generally skinned, and the skins stretched and sewn onto models. In the case of *fish* and *reptiles,* because of the changeability and tendency of the skins to crack, artificial reproductions made from the original animals are frequently developed. These are usually more lifelike and always more durable than the real skins would be.

A general procedure in all taxidermy is to take accurate measurements of all parts of the body, and detailed notes on the colors of parts, eyes, and so on. Later these are needed for adding the final realistic touches.

Small mammals and birds are similarly treated. They are cleaned of debris. The skin is carefully separated from the body, usually by being cut from the ventral side. The bones are fleshed and cleaned for display or other use. Chemicals, such as powdered borax, are rubbed on bird skins as they are stripped, in order to preserve them. The skin is later water-washed and treated for preservation. In the same way, small mammal skins are cleaned and tanned. This permits them to endure indefinitely.

Balsa models are prepared from dimensions of the original animal. Padding of various materials is used where necessary. The skin is stretched over the form. Wire is used to support birds' wings and other parts. Glass eyes are used in place of natural ones. Final fluffing of feathers or fur and touching up with colors and it is ready for display.

In the preparation of larger mammals, a different procedure is necessary. Molds of plaster of Paris are often made directly, in addition to the taking of measurements from the freshly killed animal. These aid later in giving the specimen a natural appearance. The skin is carefully removed. The skin is salted to preserve it, and left a few days before it is tanned. The bones are stripped of muscles and cleaned to be used in displays or for other purposes. When ready, the bones are assembled as they were in the living animal. A clay model which duplicates the original animal body is made around the skeleton. This leaves a good but clumsy, heavy specimen. Around this is made a plaster mold. When dry, sections of it are separated. Layers of burlap are glued in, and iron rods are anchored within to provide later support. This forms what is called the *mannikin.* It is well made since it will be the specimen's final body. The molds are wired together and the mannikin within is allowed to dry for a few days. When it is ready, the mold is cut and broken away. The mannikin is then sewn together and finished. The skin is stretched and sewn over it, and final arranging and positioning are done.

In the case of fish, several procedures are used. The earlier one involved skinning of the fish and building a model of the body. An alternative was to use a mold of the original fish (by making a plaster cast), over which was stretched the skin. This gives a good specimen except that in passing years the skin may crack. A preferable method is to make casts in plaster from molds taken of the original fish. These, when painted realistically, are a durable and accurate, if artificial, representation of the original.

Reptiles are sometimes prepared as fish are. There is a better method which is used for many of them, as well as for other kinds of animals. It is especially effective where color has to show through *translucently* from within. Many animals with bare skin like snakes, turkey heads, or *hippopotami,* have in real life a color quality which disappears in skin preparation. A plastic model is made of them. First, a plaster cast is made of parts or of the whole dead animal. It is done with extreme care, with the animal's position as it is desired for final display. The sections are then separated. With infinite care, liquid plastic is applied to the inside of the mold. (Imagine painting a water glass from within.) Appropriate colors are added to the plastic and painted on. This is a painstaking task since the building up of color layers takes place gradually. Because the color layers are applied from the model's inside, each layer will show through as the final coloration of the animal.

When all colored plastic is layered in, a center filler is put in for strength. After drying, the outside plaster mold is wet and broken away. This method gives the most realistic results for reptiles.   D. J. I.

Taxonomy see Anatomy; Animals, classification of; Evolution; Plants, classification of

REINFORCING RODS AND BOARDS FORM THE PRIMARY SKELETON OR FOUNDATION TO SIMULATE THE GORILLA

THE BODY IS THEN BUILT UP AND FASHIONED WITH CLAY. WHEN WELL-ROUNDED AND LIFE-LIKE IN SIZE, THE SKIN IS FITTED FOR SIZE AND REMOVED

NEXT A COAT OF CLAY IS PLACED OVER THE MOLD, ALLOWED TO DRY AND THEN CUT OFF IN SECTIONS AND REINFORCED AND BRACED

WHEN THE REINFORCED PLASTER LIKENESS IS ASSEMBLED, THE SKIN IS GLUED IN PLACE

Tea Tea is an evergreen shrub or tree grown for its leaves. When they are dried and put into hot water, they make a beverage. Tea is native to the Orient and was first used as medicine. It is now grown in some of the southern states. The tea family includes the flowering CAMELLIA. The scientific name of the family is *Theaceae.*

The tea plant grows from 5 to 30 feet (1.5 to 9.1 meters), depending on pruning. The leaves are 2 to 5 inches (5 to 12.7 centimeters) long, serrated, leathery, and possessing oil glands. The flower is white to pink and develops into a capsule fruit.

The kind and quality of tea depends on several factors. The new young leaves make the best drink, called *golden tips* and *orange pekoe.* The larger leaves produce a poorer grade. The older the plant, the more bitter the leaves become. Green tea is made from dried,

Tea leaves are picked, then dried or fermented

rolled green leaves. If these same leaves were permitted to ferment, black tea would be produced.

Tea contains three useful chemicals—*essential oil, tannin* and *theine*. The last one is a stimulant. When tea is brewed too long, the tannin dissolves and is freed, making the tea bitter.   H. J. C.

SEE ALSO: ECONOMIC BOTANY

Teak (TEEK) The teak is a tall, large, tropical tree well-known for its strong wood. The teak wood contains a fragrant oil that preserves wood and metals from rust and decay. Teakwood is used in shipbuilding, furniture, and in making chests and beautifully carved ornaments.

Teak trees grow to 200 feet (61 meters) tall. Oval, simple leaves may be 12 inches long (30 centimeters) long. A red or purple dye can be made from them. Teak flowers are small and perfect, having both male and female parts. The petals are united.

Teak is native to Southeast Asia. The wood is rare and expensive because of the difficulty in lumbering it. Elephants in India, Burma, and Thailand are used to harvest teak logs. This tree belongs in the family Verbenaceae.   H. J. C.

Teal see Duck

Wood of the teak tree has an attractive grain

Tears Tears are a watery liquid bathing the eyeball. They keep the surface of the eyeball moist and clean. Tears are always being produced and drained away. They drain through the nose (*nasolacrimal canal*) from ducts (*lacrimal*) at the corner of the eye nearest the nose. In weeping so many tears are produced at one time that they do not drain away fast enough and spill out of the eye.

SEE: EYE

Technetium (teck-NEE-shih-um) Technetium is a chemical element. It is not radioactively stable, that is, it does not have a stable ISOTOPE and, like PROMETHIUM, is not found in Nature. Technetium was formerly called *masurium*.

Technetium is related to MANGANESE and RHENIUM, and is in the same group in the periodic table. Thus chemically, it behaves like these elements. It has metallic properties. Technetium is produced by nuclear bombardment of MOLYBDENUM atoms or as a *fission* product of uranium-235.

Technetium (symbol Tc) has atomic number 43. Its most stable isotope has mass number 97. It forms compounds with oxygen, and most of its radioactive isotopes have very short half-lives.   D.J.I.

SEE ALSO: ATOM, ELEMENTS

Technicolor see Motion pictures

Technology Technology is applied science and industrial art. It takes the discoveries and inventions of scientists and makes them available in practical form for man. It supplies the needs of mankind with tools and machines.

Through mass production, machines produce goods faster and cheaper and, in many instances, better than can be made by hand. A machine, driven by steam, electric, or atomic energy can make products which cannot be produced by hand. Synthetic dyes, drugs, foods, clothes, fuels, cars, airplanes, and ships are only a very few products made possible by technology.   D. A. B.

SEE ALSO: SCIENCE

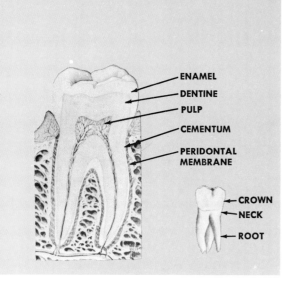

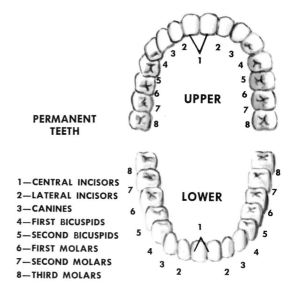

PERMANENT
TEETH

1—CENTRAL INCISORS
2—LATERAL INCISORS
3—CANINES
4—FIRST BICUSPIDS
5—SECOND BICUSPIDS
6—FIRST MOLARS
7—SECOND MOLARS
8—THIRD MOLARS

UPPER

LOWER

TODAY'S HEALTH, published by AMERICAN MEDICAL ASSOCIATION

Teeth All mammals use their teeth to chew food. Many other animals also have these bony organs in their mouth. Teeth may be used to grab, hold and tear food. They may serve for protection, such as the poison fangs of a rattlesnake. The walrus uses its tusks to drag its body along rocky shores. Beavers use their sharp teeth to cut down trees to build homes. Some animals are toothless. Birds, toads, turtles, some fish and a small community of men in India do not have a tooth in their heads.

Humans have two sets of teeth. *Baby,* or *temporary,* teeth begin to appear in about the sixth month. By the time a child is two years old, he usually has all twenty. The second set, or *permanent teeth,* are buried in the gums beneath the temporary ones. At this stage they are much smaller than they will be eventually. When the child is about six years old, the permanent teeth begin to push the baby teeth out. This process will continue for six years (twenty years for wisdom teeth) until an adult has 32 permanent teeth. The *dental formula* (2-1-2-3) refers to the number of kind of teeth in each one half of each jaw. Man has two *incisors,* one *canine,* two *bicuspids,* and three *molars.*

Though teeth vary in size and shape, their internal structure is similar. The *crown* is that portion extending out from the gums. It is composed of *dentine,* a dense bony material, which is covered by hard *enamel.* The crown tapers to the *neck* and finally into one or more hollow roots. The opening at the base of the root permits blood vessels and nerves to enter the pulp cavity.

The proper development of teeth depends upon numerous factors. Since the composition of teeth is high in calcium, phosphorus and other minerals, the diet of an animal is very important. Vitamins A, B, D are essential. FLUORINE is helpful in maintaining clean and healthy teeth. An insufficient supply of hormones from some endocrine glands, THYROID and PARATHYROID, will affect the normal growth of strong teeth. Certain chemicals will cause the calcium salts in enamel to become soluble and start decay. One such action will occur when bacteria digest carbohydrates and give off acids.

Teeth aid the whole process of digestion. Chewing food makes it easier to swallow and adds moisture to dry foods. It permits the saliva carrying the enzyme *amylase* to become thoroughly mixed with the food.

Teeth have been part of the animal body almost from the beginning of animal life. Among the invertebrates, the HOOKWORM has platelike teeth to help suck blood. The teeth of CHITON in leeches help obtain food from their hosts. Snails have a radula of teeth to scrape plants. Crayfish have teeth in their stomachs that are used for grinding. Mammals have two sets and a definite number of teeth. Rodents' teeth are open at the base of the root to allow for continued growth. They keep wearing them down from constant gnawing. Most of the teeth of pigs are present at birth. The largest tooth was in an extinct mammoth. It was 16 feet (4.9 meters) long and weighed over 250 pounds (113 kilograms). H.J.C.

SEE ALSO: TOOTH DECAY

Tektites Tektites are generally small, rounded, black to greenish glassy objects. Many scientists believe that tektites may have originated in outer space and fallen to earth. But this theory has not been proved.

Tektites resemble OBSIDIAN, but have different chemical compositions generally containing 70-80 percent SILICA. Most tektites are button- or teardrop-shaped and may be grooved or pitted on their surfaces. These features tend to suggest that they have been completely melted. They show aerodynamic sculpturing, which also suggests high-speed passage through the earth's atmosphere.

Tektites are found throughout the world in concentrations called *strewnfields*. They are primarily found in Southeast Asia, Australia, West Africa, Czechoslovakia, and isolated locations in Texas and Georgia. Microtektites are also found in deep-sea sediments. The youngest strewnfields apparently formed about 700,000 years ago, and the oldest about 32 million years ago. Their origin is still a mystery. They appear to be the result of perhaps a *meteorite* impact, because tektite-like objects were found around the impact craters on the moon. Some believe they may have formed during volcanic eruptions or meteorite impacts on earth.   P.P.S.

SEE ALSO: METEOR, MOON

Telegraph Telegraph is an instrument of communication. Messages are sent and received by signals made by connecting and breaking an electric circuit. Before telegraphy, messages could not be sent quickly.

There are basically two kinds of telegraphy—*line* or *wire telegraphy* and *wireless* or *radiotelegraphy*. In wire telegraphy the sending and receiving stations are connected by a direct wire. In radiotelegraphy, the telegraph signals are sent out from a special RADIO transmitter and picked up on a special radio receiver. There is no wire connecting the sending and receiving stations. Wire telegraphy is used by the Western Union system, by railroads, by large companies which have direct wires between branch offices, and by the military services. Radiotelegraphy is used for ship-to-shore communication, in military installations, and by shortwave radio amateurs.

The wire telegraph originally consisted of a *sending key,* which opened and closed the circuit, and a *sounder* connected by wires to the key. The voltage was supplied by a battery. When the circuit was closed by the key, an iron bar was attracted in the electromagnet of the sounder. When the circuit was opened, the bar was pulled away by a spring. When the bar hit the electromagnet, it produced a click. These clicks were varied according to the *Morse code.*

Although key circuits are still used in places, most wire lines are *teletypewriter* lines. Both sending and receiving points have a device which resembles a typewriter, but the keyboard only has capitals and numerals on it. The message is typed on this teletypewriter, which automatically transmits each letter as a series of pulses. A different pulse pattern represents each letter, much as a different combination of dots and dashes represents each letter in code.

The receiving unit converts the electrical pulses back to mechanical energy and the message is automatically typed out.

When the same message must be sent to many receivers, a unit is used which perforates a paper tape. This perforated tape is inserted into a device which converts the perforations into electrical pulses to be sent over wire or fed to a radio transmitter.

In radiotelegraphy, the transmitted wave is modulated (altered) so it can carry a message. Modulation is imposed by opening and closing a circuit, either by a key or with a teletypewriter tape.

The telegraph was not the contribution of one man. One of the contributors was James Maxwell, who, in 1831, studied and clarified the theory of *electromagnetism*. He and a German scientist, Henry Hertz, experimented with electromagnetic waves. An inventor named David Hughes learned to detect electromagnetic waves, using a gap in his spark transmitter. In 1831, MICHAEL FARADAY discovered *electrical inductance.* Later, the Italian electrical engineer MARCONI improved the wireless telegraph so that it would transmit signals for longer distances.

Two Americans, JOSEPH HENRY and Samuel F. Morse, also contributed greatly to the development of the telegraph. E. Y. K.

SEE ALSO: ELECTROMAGNET; INDUCTION; MORSE, SAMUEL

※ **THINGS TO DO**

SENDING MESSAGES BY CODE

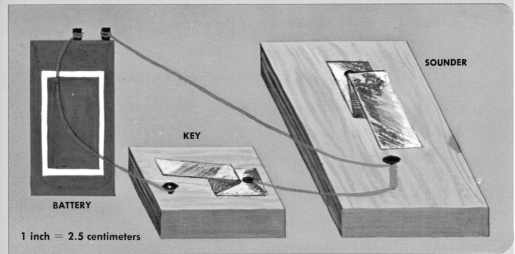

SOUNDER

KEY

BATTERY

1 inch = 2.5 centimeters

1 Assemble an electromagnet by wrapping bell wire around a screw at least twenty turns. Screw the electromagnet into a small board.

2 Cut a strip of metal from a tin can. Make it one inch wide and two inches longer than the length of the screw. This will serve as the armature when fastened near the electromagnet. Follow the diagram. You have just constructed a telegraph sounder.

3 Assemble a telegraph key or switch with a second small board, screw, and metal strip. Bend the key upwards as shown in the illustration.

4 The two free ends of bell wire leading from the telegraph sounder should be connected to the screw on the switch and to one terminal on the dry cell. A third wire connects the other terminal to the screw holding the key.

5 Learn the Morse code from the table below and with a friend send messages back and forth.

INTERNATIONAL MORSE CODE

A ·—	N —·	1 ·————	6 —····
B —···	O ———	2 ··———	7 ——···
C —·—·	P ·——·	3 ···——	8 ———··
D —··	Q ——·—	4 ····—	9 ————·
E ·	R ·—·	5 ·····	0 —————
F ··—·	S ···		
G ——·	T —		
H ····	U ··—	Period ·—·—·—	
I ··	V ···—	Comma ——··——	
J ·———	W ·——	SOS ···———···	
K —·—	X —··—	Start —·—	
L ·—··	Y —·——	End of message ·—·—·	
M ——	Z ——··	Error ········	

Alexander Graham Bell and his original model of the telephone

Telephone Since Alexander Bell invented the telephone in 1876, it has become the most important means of COMMUNICATION. It can send the sound of a voice to any receiver on the same line, and the line from a telephone can be connected to almost any telephone in the world. RADIO and TELEVISION networks use telephone lines to send their programs between stations. The telephone system uses radio to send calls overseas to any country with a telephone system.

The telephone sends and receives sound on wires, or lines, by changing the sound to electric pulses. The telephone headset has a *receiver* and a *transmitter*. The transmitter that Bell used in his first working telephone was crude. The same method has been refined and is used in modern telephones to change sound vibrations into electric impulses. Bell knew that sound vibrations could produce similar vibrations in any solid object. He experimented with a thin metal reed attached to a simple switch. The switch was connected to a battery and a receiver. He found that this transmitter could not send a human voice, and he looked for another method of controlling the battery current.

He attached a thin metal *diaphragm* to a tiny box filled with carbon granules. The carbon box was connected so that it completed the telephone line circuit back to the battery.

Carbon black, or soot, is a poor conductor used in *resistors;* but it can be finely divided. It will conduct better when it is compressed than when it is loosely packed. In Bell's transmitter, the diaphragm is alternately pushed and pulled by the sound vibrations; and the carbon granules are pushed closer together and farther apart in the same way. The diaphragm simply acts as a sound-sensitive surface, but the carbon box actually changes the battery current into electric pulses that copy the sound impulses. The important difference between the carbon telephone transmitter and the simple switch that Bell discarded is that the switch turns the current completely on or off, while his ingenious carbon box could change the current continuously from zero to maximum. It could send a sound which has several frequencies, such as the complex human voice.

In reproducing a voice, Bell used another principle. He used electromagnets in a receiver to change the electric pulses back into sound. He connected the electromagnet coils to the telephone line, and mounted a diaphragm at one end of the coils so that it could vibrate slightly. When current flowed in the electromagnet, the steel diaphragm pulled toward it, and was released when the current stopped. In this way the diaphragm vibrated to reproduce the sound picked up by the transmitter.

In a system with more than two sets of transmitters and receivers, some switching system must be used to send a call to a selected station. In the modern telephone

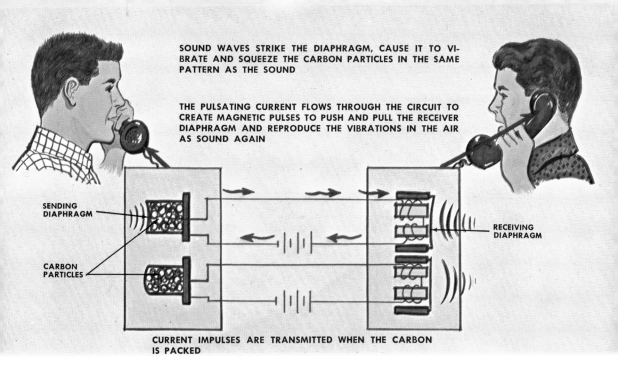

SOUND WAVES STRIKE THE DIAPHRAGM, CAUSE IT TO VIBRATE AND SQUEEZE THE CARBON PARTICLES IN THE SAME PATTERN AS THE SOUND

THE PULSATING CURRENT FLOWS THROUGH THE CIRCUIT TO CREATE MAGNETIC PULSES TO PUSH AND PULL THE RECEIVER DIAPHRAGM AND REPRODUCE THE VIBRATIONS IN THE AIR AS SOUND AGAIN

SENDING DIAPHRAGM

CARBON PARTICLES

RECEIVING DIAPHRAGM

CURRENT IMPULSES ARE TRANSMITTED WHEN THE CARBON IS PACKED

system, switches are the most numerous components. The vast system of lines, relays, crossbar switches, and computers took more than 50 years to develop. All calls are switched through two types of offices—the local, or exchange, office; and the regional office, which handles the interexchange and long distance calls. Most exchange offices now use an automatic dialing system instead of an operator, but a few rural areas still use manual switching.

Before 1913, the first dialing systems were used by small independent companies. By 1930, the Bell Telephone dialing system automatically connected phones within the exchange areas. The long-distance calls were relayed from exchange to exchange by operators using trunk lines. Now, any number in the United States can be directly dialed if the exchange has been connected into the direct dialing trunks.   D. A. B.

SEE ALSO: BELL, ALEXANDER GRAHAM; ELECTROMAGNET; SOUND; VOICE

Telephotography In telephotography, photographs are "sensed" by a system of photoelectric cells as a light beam is scanned across them. Depending upon the brightness of the reflected light, a current can be amplified and sent over wire circuits or radio. Long range lenses, *telescopes,* enable photographs to be made on film.

SEE: PHOTOELECTRICITY, PHOTOGRAPHY

Principle of telephotography

FACSIMILE

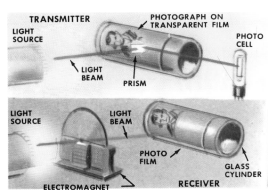

TRANSMITTER

LIGHT SOURCE

PHOTOGRAPH ON TRANSPARENT FILM

PHOTO CELL

LIGHT BEAM

PRISM

LIGHT SOURCE

LIGHT BEAM

PHOTO FILM

GLASS CYLINDER

ELECTROMAGNET

RECEIVER

✳ **THINGS TO DO**

MAKING A REFRACTING TELESCOPE

1   Locate two long cardboard tubes, one slightly smaller in circumference.

2   Two lens (one of long focal length and one of short) are needed which match the diameter of the tubes. Fasten one in the opposite end of each tube.

3   When the smaller tube is placed into the larger tube you are ready to observe. Move the smaller tube in and out until the object is clear.

4   Is the picture upside down? Use your telescope at night. Can you see stars better than with the naked eye?

Telescope A telescope is an instrument that is used to observe and study distant objects. It is one of the most important tools of the astronomer.

The main function of a telescope is to bring into view objects that are so faint they cannot be seen with the naked eye. Telescopes also magnify distant objects. They can separate objects, such as double stars, that are so close together that they appear as one to the naked eye, and more detail can be seen on distant objects.

The telescope consists of a long tube holding lenses, or mirrors and lenses, the proper distances apart to collect light waves from a distant object and form a visible image of it.

There are two main types of telescopes: *refracting* telescopes and *reflecting* telescopes. In a refracting telescope, a large *convex* lens is situated at the top of a long tube. This "object glass" collects the nearly parallel light waves from a distant object and bends, or refracts, the waves to form an image farther down inside the tube. A simple experiment with a magnifying glass shows how this principle of refraction works. If a magnifying glass (a lens) is held a few inches away from a piece of paper so that the sun shines directly on the lens, an image of the sun will be formed on the paper. In a telescope this image is not focused on a screen for viewing by the eye. Instead, another lens, the *eyepiece,* is situated at the bottom of the tube. The eyepiece magnifies the image formed within the tube by the object glass and focuses the light waves into the image that the observer sees.

Reflecting telescopes use *mirrors* to *reflect* light instead of lenses that refract it. A re-

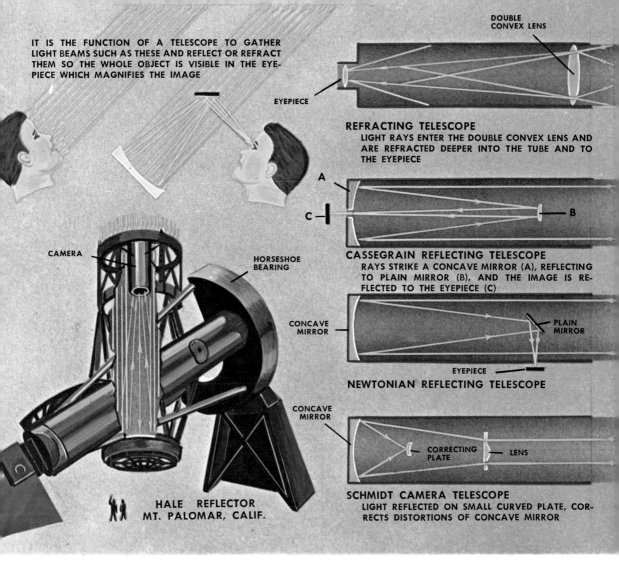

IT IS THE FUNCTION OF A TELESCOPE TO GATHER LIGHT BEAMS SUCH AS THESE AND REFLECT OR REFRACT THEM SO THE WHOLE OBJECT IS VISIBLE IN THE EYEPIECE WHICH MAGNIFIES THE IMAGE

EYEPIECE

DOUBLE CONVEX LENS

REFRACTING TELESCOPE
LIGHT RAYS ENTER THE DOUBLE CONVEX LENS AND ARE REFRACTED DEEPER INTO THE TUBE AND TO THE EYEPIECE

A

C

B

CASSEGRAIN REFLECTING TELESCOPE
RAYS STRIKE A CONCAVE MIRROR (A), REFLECTING TO PLAIN MIRROR (B), AND THE IMAGE IS REFLECTED TO THE EYEPIECE (C)

CAMERA

HORSESHOE BEARING

CONCAVE MIRROR

PLAIN MIRROR

EYEPIECE

NEWTONIAN REFLECTING TELESCOPE

CONCAVE MIRROR

CORRECTING PLATE

LENS

HALE REFLECTOR MT. PALOMAR, CALIF.

SCHMIDT CAMERA TELESCOPE
LIGHT REFLECTED ON SMALL CURVED PLATE, CORRECTS DISTORTIONS OF CONCAVE MIRROR

flecting telescope consists of a large hollow tube at the bottom of which is a *concave* mirror. The mirror reflects the light waves and focuses them in an image near the top of the tube. A second, plain mirror reflects this image so that it can be seen with the eyepiece near the top of the telescope.

The degree of magnification of a telescope is determined by the *focal length* of the eyepiece and by the focal length of the objective lens. There is a practical limit to the degree of magnification of any telescope. The larger the objective lens, the greater the magnification that can be achieved without fuzziness.

The world's largest reflecting telescope is at the Keck Observatory on Mauna Kea, Hawaii. The mirror is 400 inches (10 meters) wide, and is composed of 36 hexagonal segments. The Keck telescope was completed in 1992 by the California Institute of Technology and the University of California. The largest refractor (40 inches, or 102 centime-

ters) is at Yerkes Observatory in Wisconsin.

The refracting telescope was invented around 1600 by Hans Lippershey, an eyeglass maker from Holland. GALILEO was the first person to use the refracting telescope to study the heavens. James Gregory worked out the principle of the reflecting telescope in 1663. About five years later SIR ISAAC NEWTON built a reflecting telescope.

In 1931 the RADIO TELESCOPE was developed by Karl Jansky, who discovered that radio signals come to earth from outer space. The radio telescope permits the mapping of gas-clouded sections of the sky. The radio telescope led to the discovery of QUASARS.

In 1990 the SPACE SHUTTLE launched the Hubble Space Telescope. With the space telescope, astronomers will be able to see up to ten times as far as they can with earthbased telescopes, without the distortions caused by earth's atmosphere. Special cameras and other sophisticated instruments will gather data in the ultraviolet, visible, and near-infrared regions of the spectrum. The space telescope will be able to operate in daylight.

D.D.

SEE ALSO: ASTRONOMY; LENS, MAN-MADE; OBSERVATORY; QUASAR; RADIO TELESCOPE

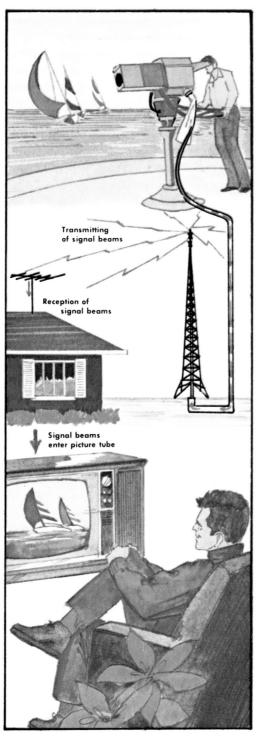

Transmitting
of signal beams

Reception of
signal beams

Signal beams
enter picture tube

Television Television is the system of electronically reproducing visual images. In many respects, the television process is similar to that of the motion picture. In television, however, electron tubes replace the photographic film of the motion picture.

The television process may be described as three principal steps: a scene is recorded with a camera, the images are transmitted on radio waves or special cables, and the receiver converts the electronic images to a picture for viewing. Normally, sound is also transmitted as radio waves with the pictures. However, for certain industrial applications, sound is not required.

TELEVISION CAMERA

The television camera is made up of a lens system, a camera tube, and various electronic circuits. Because these components are so bulky and heavy, the camera is usually mounted on some type of movable stand or tripod.

The lens system focuses the light rays of the scene on the face of the camera tube. Usually, several lenses of varying magnification can be selected and quickly positioned to record closeup or distant objects.

The *image orthicon* tube is the most widely used camera tube because of its extremely high sensitivity and adaptability to changing light conditions. It consists of three main parts: the screen, the target, and the electron gun. When the scene is focused upon the light-sensitive screen, *photoelectrons* are emitted and flow towards the target. When the photoelectrons hit the target, additional electrons are knocked off the target, leaving it with a positive charge at that point. Bright light focused from white objects produces a heavy flow of electrons to the target, while weaker light focused from the dark areas produces a weak flow of electrons. The target, therefore, forms an electronic image of the recorded scene. The entire target image cannot be transmitted all at one time.

The *electron gun* is a device which scans tiny sections of the target very rapidly, sending strong or weak electronic impulses to the transmitter depending upon the strength of the charge on the target. A beam of electrons emitted from the gun moves from the left to right across the target. At the end of

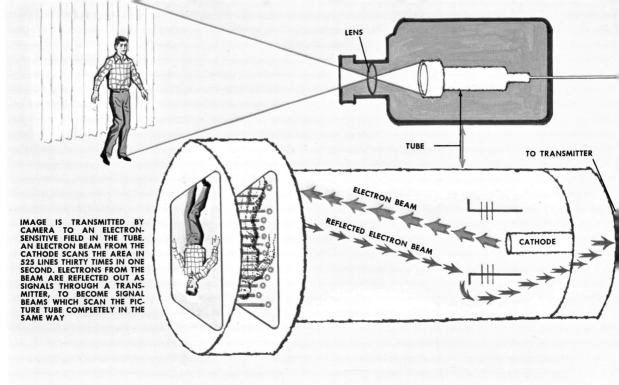

LENS

TUBE

TO TRANSMITTER

ELECTRON BEAM

REFLECTED ELECTRON BEAM

CATHODE

IMAGE IS TRANSMITTED BY CAMERA TO AN ELECTRON-SENSITIVE FIELD IN THE TUBE. AN ELECTRON BEAM FROM THE CATHODE SCANS THE AREA IN 525 LINES THIRTY TIMES IN ONE SECOND. ELECTRONS FROM THE BEAM ARE REFLECTED OUT AS SIGNALS THROUGH A TRANSMITTER, TO BECOME SIGNAL BEAMS WHICH SCAN THE PICTURE TUBE COMPLETELY IN THE SAME WAY

each sweep, the beam returns to the left but moves a fraction of an inch lower.

This process is repeated until the entire picture is scanned from the upper left to the lower right corner. Two separate scans, called *interlace scanning,* are made to cover the whole image. The first, third, fifth, etc., horizontal lines are swept first, then the second, fourth, sixth, etc., lines are swept to complete the picture. Federal Communications Commission regulations require that an image be scanned with 525 lines at the rate of 30 pictures per second. The scanning beam, therefore, moves horizontally in less than 1/15,000 of a second, completing the odd-line scan in 1/60 of a second.

Electrons emitted from the gun are returned to the circuit after striking the target. If the beam hits a highly charged spot (bright area), the positive charge attracts the electrons and fewer electrons are returned. If a low charged spot (dark area) is hit, more electrons are bounced back. These returning electron pulses carry the picture information to the transmitter where they are combined with the signals needed to keep the camera tube and receiver picture tube synchronized (in step).

TELEVISION TRANSMITTER

The transmitter is a special RADIO wave generator which sends the video signals through the air. A high-energy electromagnetic wave (carrier) generated by the transmitter is changed in shape by the addition of the varying video signals. The resulting modulated wave is of very high or ultrahigh frequency and can normally be received only to the horizon, about 150 miles (240 kilometers). To attain maximum reception, television broadcasting and receiver antennas are placed as high as possible.

Microwave towers, placed every 30 miles (48 kilometers), receive, amplify, and relay the transmitted signals over long distances by changing them to microwave radio signals. *Coaxial cables,* used for long-distance communications, are employed for nationwide transmission of television signals.

Video signals are transmitted on one of 12 Very High Frequency (VHF) or 70 Ultra High Frequency (UHF) channels.

TELEVISION RECEIVER

The television receiver reverses the process of the transmitter and camera so that a picture can be viewed. An antenna intercepts the weak modulated carrier wave and feeds it to the electronic components of the receiver set. The video signal is amplified and separated from the carrier wave on which it was transmitted. The video signal is then converted to varying electronic impulses just like those that left the camera. These signals are fed to the controls of the receiving *cathode ray tube,* also called the *kinescope* or *picture* tube. The kinescope reverses the action of the image orthicon. The beam from the electron gun of the kinescope scans the fluorescent screen at the same rate as the

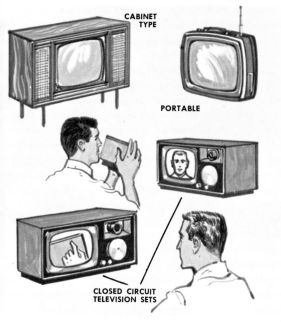

CABINET TYPE

PORTABLE

CLOSED CIRCUIT TELEVISION SETS

camera scanning beam. As the beam of electrons scans the fluorescent face of the screen, light and dark areas made up of tiny dots appear in direct relationship to the intensity of the video signals controlling emission from the gun. Because the scanning rate is so fast and the fluorescent dots continue to glow for a short period of time, persistence of vision makes the whole picture appear to be projected at one time.

COLOR TELEVISION

Thus far, only equipment involving *monochrome,* or black and white, signals has been mentioned. *Color* television is actually transmitted as black and white signals with the following differences. Three image orthicon tubes are required in the television camera, each sensitive to only one color—red, blue, or green. The three different electronic impulses are combined and broadcast as one signal. The color television receiver contains a picture tube with three electron guns, one for each color, and a special phosphor-coated screen. The phosphors are tiny clusters of dots, each cluster containing dots which glow red, blue, or green when excited by their respective electron-beam flow. Because of their closeness, the primary colored dots cannot be seen separately, but appear to blend into the color of the original scene. Color broadcasts can also be seen in black and white since a special black and white signal is required with color transmissions.

CABLE AND SATELLITE TELEVISION

During the 1970s and 1980s, companies developed systems that delivered television signals over coaxial CABLES to subscribers in cities and towns. By the late 1980s, more than half of all U.S. households subscribed to paid cable television. In 1975, the first satellite designed to receive and transmit television signals was put into orbit by RCA. The development of communication satellites prompted the formation of dozens of new television networks, including Home Box Office, Cable News Network, and, in Europe, Rupert Murdoch's Sky Channel.

Cable television companies are able to receive satellite-transmitted signals by means of a satellite receiving dish, also called an *earth station.* Once the signal is received, it is amplified and distributed to households on coaxial cable. In the 1980s, the popularity of home satellite dishes increased. For a few thousand dollars, individuals could install a miniature earth station and receive the same signals intended for cable company earth stations. In 1986, some satellite networks began scrambling their signals so programming could only be seen after expensive decoders were installed. Many communication experts foresee Direct Broadcast Satellite (DBS) systems installed in homes as the wave of television's future. By the early 1990s, DBS networks were gaining popularity in Europe and Japan. High-definition television (HDTV), a standard producing sharper pictures, is also gaining acceptance.   E.I.D./J.H.

SEE ALSO: ANTENNA; CATHODE-RAY TUBE; ELECTRONICS; PERSISTENCE OF VISION; PHOTOELECTRICITY; SATELLITE, MAN-MADE; VHF

Tellurium (teh-LOOR-ee-um) Tellurium (element 52) is a scarce element, possessing some metallic properties. In its pure form it is found in igneous rock in Colorado, Bolivia, and Europe. J. F. M. von Reichenstein first isolated tellurium in 1782.

Tellurium (symbol Te) has atomic weight 127.60. In crystalline form, it is a silvery-white, brittle metal. In its amorphous form, it is brownish-gray powder.

Gold is chemically inactive but unites readily with tellurium to form gold tellurides, important ores.

Tellurium is used to improve the ductility of steel, as a dye in glass, as an additive in lead alloys, and as catalysts for cracking petroleum.   I. K. F.

SEE ALSO: ELEMENTS

Telophase see Mitosis and meiosis

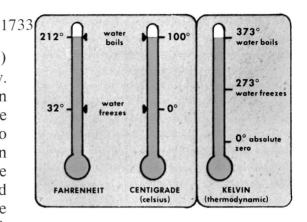

Temperature (TEM-per-uh-tchoor) One deals with temperature every day. For example, the average person needs to know about the temperature of the air in order to know what to wear. The temperature of the air on the earth varies over a wide range. The highest temperature ever recorded was 136.4° F. (58° C.) in Libya. The lowest temperature of -126.7° F. (-88.3° C.) was recorded at a Russian weather station in Antarctica.

Every object holds some heat, down to a temperature called *absolute zero,* which is -273.16° C. or -459.69° F. The theory is that below this temperature molecules cease to move. The temperatures of objects are useful in science to understand the properties of materials and use them better. The scientist relates temperature to the *average kinetic energy* of the molecules of any substance containing *heat* energy.   E.Y.K.
SEE ALSO: ABSOLUTE ZERO, MOLECULAR THEORY

Temperature scales The temperature of different materials can be measured in different scales. Three common temperature scales are used today. They are called the Fahrenheit, Centigrade (Celsius), and the Absolute or Kelvin. All three scales are based on the freezing and boiling points of water at sea level.

The common household and fever thermometers use the Fahrenheit scale with the freezing point of 32° F. and the boiling point at 212° F. Healthy body temperature is between 98.0° and 99.0° Fahrenheit.

The Centigrade or Celsius scale is used in many countries. Its FREEZING POINT is 0° C. and its BOILING POINT 100° C.; therefore, there are 100 divisions between the freezing and the boiling points of water.

Temperatures in Fahrenheit may be converted to Centigrade temperatures, and vice versa, by using the following formulas:
$$C = 5/9 \ (F - 32)$$
$$F = 9/5 \ (C + 32)$$

In the Absolute or Kelvin scale, zero degrees is at absolute zero, -273.16° C. There are 100 divisions between the freezing point and boiling point of water, so conversion from the Absolute scale to the Centigrade scale is easy:
$$A = C + 273.16$$
$$C = A - 273.16$$

The Kelvin scale is also known as the thermodynamic scale. The thermodynamic scale is used to define temperature in the INTERNATIONAL SYSTEM OF UNITS (SI). This temperature scale is used for expressing very high temperatures in astronomy and physics. Star temperatures range from 25,000 K. to 3,500 K. It is also used in low-temperature physics, CRYOGENICS. The boiling point for liquid air is 83 K. and 4.2 K. for helium.

An absolute scale based on Fahrenheit, the way Kelvin is based on Centigrade, is sometimes used. It is called the *Rankine* scale. On it, water freezes at 491.7°.   E.Y.K.
SEE ALSO: ABSOLUTE ZERO, TEMPERATURE, THERMOMETER

Tempering Tempering is heating steel or iron to a precise temperature, then quickly cooling it to produce a material of greater toughness.

Tendon see Anatomy, Fibrous tissue

Tendon of Achilles The tendon of Achilles is the white, fibrous cord which connects the muscle of the calf of the leg with the heel bone.

Tendril A tendril is a thin, leafless modification of a plant STEM (in the case of the grapevine) or a leaf (in the case of the pea). It attaches to an object, giving the plant support.

Tensile strength Tensile strength is the minimum STRESS a substance can bear without pulling apart.

Tentacle (TENN-tuh-kuhl) A tentacle is a whiplike organ for feeling, movement, or defense, found around the head or mouth of some *invertebrates*. It is also a hairlike part of a flower which receives outside stimuli.

SEE: COELENTERATA

Teratology (tair-ah-TAHL-uh-jee) Teratology is the science which studies "monsters," or abnormal formations in animals and plants. Two classes are recognized: (1) malformations—dwarfism, gigantism, absence of limbs; and (2) doubling of bodies, such as Siamese twins.

SEE: EMBRYOLOGY

Terbium (TER-bee-uhm) Terbium is the 65th element, a rare earth. It was discovered in 1842. Today it is purified and separated from the ore by electrolytic methods.

Terbium (symbol Tb) is a silvery-gray metal. It is easily oxidized in the air. The oxide, formula Tb_2O_3, is a white solid, while the peroxide, formula Tb_4O_7, is a dark solid. Nitrate and sulfate salts can also be formed. The atomic weight of terbium is 158.924.

M. S.

Termite Termites, often called *white ants*, are not really ants. They belong to an entirely different order of IN-SECTS. They are, however, social insects like ANTS and BEES. Termites eat wood with the help of some one-celled animals (PROTOZOA) that live in their intestines. Often they destroy wooden buildings or trees. Some live in wood, underground, or build nests. There are almost two thousand known species of termites.

Many tropical species build nests 20 feet (6.1 meters) tall and several feet or meters around at the base. These are usually made of sand grains glued together by a secretion. Thousands of termites live in a single nest. Different groups do different kinds of work for the colony. A group of insects spe-

A termite nest   Buchsbaun

cialized for a particular job is called a *caste*. There are three important castes—the *reproductive,* the *worker,* and the *soldier.* Unlike other social insects, there are both males and females in each caste.

Colonies are established after a nuptial flight by a winged *king* and *queen.* They shed their wings after mating. In large nests, other wingless adults may reproduce as well as the king and queen.

The worker caste consists of nymphs (*larvae*) and sterile adults. Usually the adults are pale, wingless, and blind. Workers do most of the work in the colony. They collect food and feed queens, soldiers, and newly hatched young. They also build the nest of wood and earth mixed with excrement and saliva. In those species that cultivate fungi for food, the workers care for the fungus gardens.

Soldiers are sterile individuals with large heads and jaws. They are larger than workers and often have compound eyes. Their jaws can be so large that workers have to feed them. When a colony is disturbed, the soldiers attack the intruding insects, often species of ants. Another caste among some termites, the *nasuti,* has a narrow snout through which it shoots a sticky, repellent fluid at the intruders.

J. C. K.

Tern There are about one hundred species of the gull-tern family, about half of them terns. Unlike GULLS, terns are most common on the southern and

✳ **THINGS TO DO**

MAKING AND STOCKING WOODLAND AND DESERT TERRARIUMS

A   WOODLAND TERRARIUM
A glass jar or old aquarium may be used to hold these different earth scenes. To make a woodland terrarium, spread a layer of gravel and bits of charcoal on the bottom; cover this layer with several inches or centimeters of rich garden soil. Small woodland plants, such as strawberry, fern, and moss, may be transplanted into it. Salamanders, toads, and tree frogs enjoy this kind of a world. Do not put the woodland terrarium in direct sunlight, because these plants and animals prefer shady places.

B   DESERT TERRARIUM
A desert terrarium needs sandy soil in which cacti and succulent plants are grown. Small snakes and horned toads thrive in this environment. This kind of a terrarium can use more sunlight than the others.

southeastern coasts. They are also more migratory than gulls, few wintering north of the Carolinas. Terns are *littoral* (living nearer the shore) while gulls are *pelagic* (living farther from the shoreline).

Terns eat fish, catching them by zooming headfirst into the water in the manner of a KINGFISHER. One of the best-known terns is the *common* tern. Others are: *Aleutian* tern, *Arctic* tern, *black* tern, and *Brown's* tern.

Terns are more slender than gulls and more graceful in flight. Their bills are thinner and more pointed. Terns usually point their bills down toward the water when they are searching for food. Their tails are often forked. In summer, most terns are white with a black cap extending down on the forehead. In winter, the forehead area becomes white.

Terns nest in colonies. Some species breed in inland lakes and others on sea islands. Nests may be shell-lined depressions in sand or rock or may be constructed from seaweed or grasses. Two or three eggs are laid at a time. Young terns are covered with down of a mottled pattern.   J. C. K.

Terramycin see Antibiotics

Terrapin see Turtle

Terrarium (teh-RARE-ee-um) Terrarium means "little world" and is a miniature world built to be like the place in which certain plant or animal life lives. An ant walking around in a woodland terrarium would be as small in comparison as a man walking in a forest. Setting up these little communities helps one to see and understand how plants and animals live together.

✳ **THINGS TO DO**

MAKING AND STOCKING BOG AND SEMI-AQUATIC TERRARIUMS

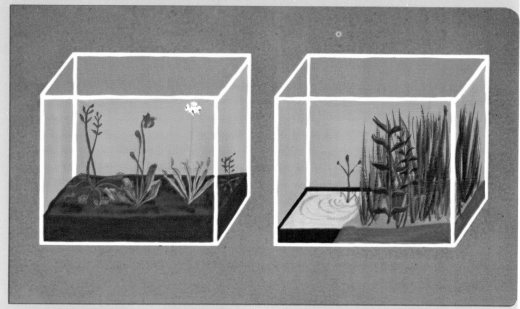

A   BOG TERRARIUM
The bottom of this terrarium should contain a mixture of one part sand, one part peat moss, and one part gravel. Bog life prefers more moisture than the other forms of life. This environment is ideal for insectivorous plants, such as the pitcher plant, sundew, and Venus' flytrap.

B   SEMI-AQUATIC TERRARIUM
The scene in this terrarium is a replica of the environment along a river bank. Place a pan at one end of the container to hold the water; the remaining section should be built up with rich soil. Small plants found on the edge of a stream may be transplanted. Aquatic bladderwort thrives in this world. Tadpoles and water insects may be kept in the water habitat.

Traveling around the country one will observe different *flora* and *fauna* in different environments. Organisms living in the dry, hot desert regions are adapted to the very high temperatures and little water. The plants and animals growing in a bog in the middle of a forest could not survive in a desert, because they need a lower temperature and more water. Before selecting the contents for a terrarium, the relationship of organisms and their environment (ECOLOGY) should be studied. The plants and animals should be placed together in the type of soil and the conditions of moisture best suited for them.   H. J. C.

Tertiary see Cenozoic Era, Geologic time table

Testa see Seed

Testis (TESS-tiss) The testis is the sex gland in the male. Within the testis, sex cells develop or mature into SPERM cells (*spermatozoa*) ready to fertilize egg cells produced by the ovaries of females. In man, maturing of sperm is controlled by *hormones* secreted by the testis and by another gland, the *pituitary,* located below the brain.

The testis consists of many coiled tubes of different widths enclosed in a connective tissue capsule. The outer capsule (*tunica albuginea*) extends partitions (*septa*) into the testis forming compartments around the tubes (*seminiferous tubules*). The tubules contain developing sperm cells and columnar-like cells called sertoli cells.

Mature sperm cells pass from the tubules into less coiled tubes or ducts known as *tubuli recti*. These tubes are lined with *columnar epithelium*.

The tubuli recti connect with still smaller ducts which make up the part of the testis called the *rete testis*. These ducts are lined with *cuboidal* or *squamous* cells bearing *flagella* on their free surfaces.

The rete ducts connect with the *vasa efferentia*, which are ducts lined with clumps of *ciliated* columnar cells alternating with flagellated cuboidal cells.

The vasa efferentia lead to the *epididymis*, a larger coiled tube similar to them in construction. After the sperm pass through all of these ducts, they finally leave the testis through the largest duct, the *vas deferens*.

J. C. K.

SEE ALSO: HISTOLOGY, MITOSIS AND MEIOSIS, REPRODUCTIVE SYSTEMS

TESTIS

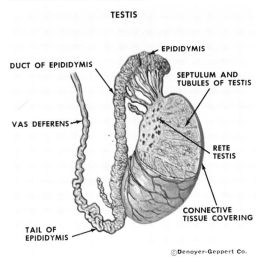

DUCT OF EPIDIDYMIS
EPIDIDYMIS
SEPTULUM AND TUBULES OF TESTIS
VAS DEFERENS
RETE TESTIS
CONNECTIVE TISSUE COVERING
TAIL OF EPIDIDYMIS
©Denoyer-Geppert Co.

Tetanus (TET-ah-nus) This is a disease of the NERVOUS SYSTEM. It is sometimes called *lockjaw* because the jaw muscles tighten and go into spasm and the mouth cannot be opened. All muscles of the body may tighten and go into CONVULSION.

Tetanus is caused by BACTERIA that enter the body through a cut or a wound. Prevention of the disease is possible by having injections of tetanus *toxoid* at regular intervals throughout life.

Tetanus results from a *toxin,* or nerve poison, produced by the tetanus bacillus (*Clostridium tetani*). The bacteria can exist for years as *spores* in soil contaminated by manure. The spores can come alive when introduced into the body. The bacteria is a slender, drumstick-shaped, mobile rod that is *anerobic,* that is, it reproduces best in the absence of oxygen. Therefore, a deep wound is more likely to develop tetanus than a slight one.

If a person develops tetanus because he has not been immunized, he is given SERUM prepared from humans who have tetanus antibodies. In addition, the wound is opened and exposed to the air. All dead tissue is cut away (*debridement*), because the bacteria will not grow in the absence of dead or dying tissue.

Medicines to relax muscles are given to prevent severe contractions (*tetany*). A tube is put into the TRACHEA to assist respiration. The surroundings are kept as quiet as possible as a sudden noise can cause intense muscle spasms throughout the body.   B. M. H.

Textile A textile is a fabric or material made by knitting, weaving, netting, or braiding natural fibers, such as COTTON, WOOL, and SILK or manmade fibers, such as NYLON, rayon, and spun glass.

SEE: SYNTHETIC FABRICS

Thalamus see Brain

Thallium (THAL-ee-um) Thallium is the 81st element. It is a heavy metal with some of the properties of lead. This element has a bluish-white color, and will leave a streak on paper as lead will. Some of its salts are sometimes used as a rat poison. The metal was discovered in 1861 by Sir William Crookes.

Thallium will oxidize easily in the air; and because it is not water soluble, it is usually kept under water to preserve its pure state. Salts, such as the chloride, the nitrate, and the oxide, have uses in organic synthesis, analytical chemistry, and glassmaking.

Thallium (symbol Tl) has atomic weight 204.37.   M. S.

SEE ALSO: ATOM, ELEMENTS

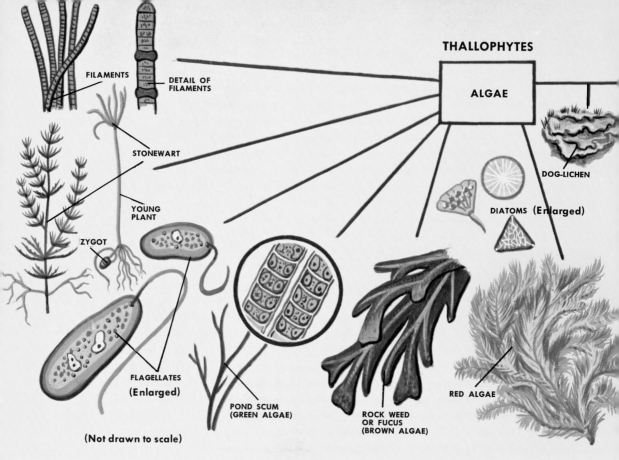

THALLOPHYTES

ALGAE

FILAMENTS — DETAIL OF FILAMENTS

STONEWART

YOUNG PLANT

ZYGOT

FLAGELLATES (Enlarged)

POND SCUM (GREEN ALGAE)

ROCK WEED OR FUCUS (BROWN ALGAE)

RED ALGAE

DIATOMS (Enlarged)

DOG-LICHEN

(Not drawn to scale)

Thallophytes (THAL-oh-fytes) Classifying plants is an old science. It is constantly changing as scientists have discovered greater differences between groups of plants. All the types of algae, fungi, and bacteria are still included by many scientists in the subkingdom Thallophyta. However, the new *taxonomic* system does not use this general title. Ten major divisions of these plants have been made.

All lack true roots, stems, leaves, flowers, fruits, or seeds. They do not possess conducting or vascular tissue. Thallophytes have very simple bodies and exhibit little cell difference.

About 110,000 species have been identified. They range in size from microscopic to giant. Some seaweeds are as long as 300 feet (91 meters). The first seven divisions are algae and make their own food. The other three divisions, with few exceptions, cannot carry on *photosynthesis.*

Division Cyanophyta Blue-green algae lack organized nuclei and plastids. They are one-celled, or unicellular, plants or aggregates of cells. They inhabit fresh and salt water, hot springs, snow, and land. No sexual reproduction has been observed in this group, the most primitive plants. The oldest fossil algae are *cyanophytes*. They possess both chlorophyll (green) and phycocyanin (bluish-green) pigments. *Nostoc, Oscillatoria,* and *Gleocapsa* are examples.

Division Chrysophyta The yellow-green algae are unicellular or colonial. Their cell walls, sometimes made of silica, often form overlapping halves. Starch is never formed. They make oil and a complicated carbohydrate. Pigments are carotenes (ruby-red color) and xanthophylls (yellowish-green). Most grow in fresh waters. *Diatoms* and *Vaucheria* are included in this group.

Division Euglenophyta Euglenoid algae are animal-like plants. They have organized chloroplastids and, many times, flexible walls. These single cells swim using one to three flagella, making them like animals. Euglenophytes live mostly in fresh water.

Division Pyrrophyta Most of the golden-brown algae are marine. They are usually unicellular, although a few grow as long filaments. They are commonly called dino-

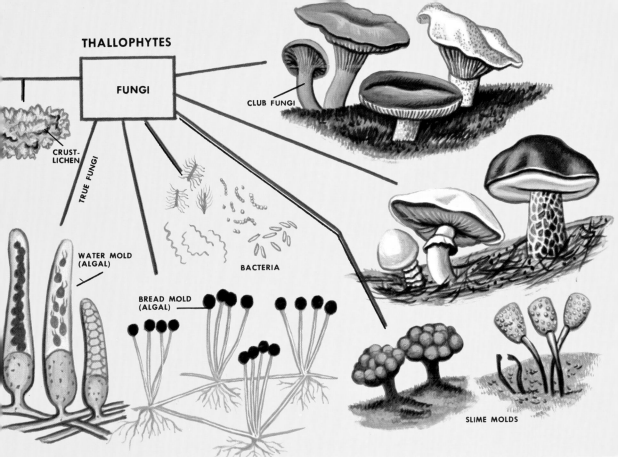

THALLOPHYTES

FUNGI

CRUST-LICHEN

TRUE FUNGI

CLUB FUNGI

WATER MOLD (ALGAL)

BACTERIA

BREAD MOLD (ALGAL)

SLIME MOLDS

flagellates because most use a whiplike appendage for locomotion. They have chlorophyll and xanthophyll pigments. Next to diatoms, they are the most numerous plankton in the sea. The red tides are caused by this group.

Division Chlorophyta Green algae probably gave rise to the present higher plants. Most live in fresh water, although some may be found in salt water or on land. They have definite nuclei and plastids and make both starch and oil. They grow as single cells, filaments, or in colonies. They possess chlorophyll and carotenoid pigments. *Spirogyra, Volvox,* and *Protococcus* are examples.

Division Rhodophyta: Most of the red algae inhabit warm marine waters. They contain chlorophyll and phycobilins (red and blue pigments). Sizes vary from small filaments to plants 4 feet (1.2 meters) tall. They manufacture a complex starch. *Nemalion* and *Polysiphonia* are in this group.

Division Phaeophyta: This group includes the multicellular brown algae. The pigment fucoxanthin (yellow) masks the green chlorophyll. They have more cell differentiation than all other algae. They range in size from small filaments to giant seaweeds hundreds of feet or meters long. *Fucus, kelp,* and *gulfweed* are typical brown algae.

Division Schizomycophyta Bacteria are the smallest living things known. They are unicellular plants without organized nuclei. Most bacteria are either SAPROPHYTES (plants that live on dead or decaying organic matter) or PARASITES (plants that live inside or upon other living organisms). Some called *purple sulfur bacteria* have a type of chlorophyll and can make their own food. Some may also use inorganic material to produce food.

Division Myxomycophyta Slime mold or slime fungus has a naked vegetative body. Cellular crosswalls and chlorophyll are absent. These plants flow like a streaming ameba. There is much doubt about their true classification and they are often called "fungus animals." Because they possess cellulose, they are plants. All are saprophytes.

Division Eumycophyta True fungi are unicellular and multicellular. Lacking chlorophyll, they are saprophytic or parasitic. Their habitat is widely diverse, but they usually grow best in shady, damp places. Most of them have bodies of two parts—the vegetative structure and a reproductive body. In most species, there is some form of sexual reproduction. There are four groups: *alga-like fungi, sac fungi, club fungi,* and *imperfect fungi.*

H. J. C.

SEE ALSO: PLANTS, CLASSIFICATION OF

Thaw Thaw means to become changed from the frozen state to the unfrozen state. It is commonly used to refer to ice and snow which melt (become fluid) when heated.
SEE: MELTING POINT

Theine see Tea

Theory A theory is an attempt to explain certain observed facts or phenomena by reasoning that they are results of other phenomena. A successful theory explains many known facts and suggests where to look for new ones.
SEE: SCIENTIFIC METHOD

Theory of relativity see Einstein, Albert; Relativity

Therapy (THER-ah-pe) Therapy is the treatment of disease. *Physiotherapy* is exercise and massage. *Chemotherapy* is treatment with drugs, and *radiotherapy* is treatment with X rays.

Thermal A thermal is a rising or descending current of air in the atmosphere. It is caused by unequal heating of the earth's surface that results in convectional currents. In flying, the so-called "air pockets" are rough air caused by thermals.
SEE ALSO: AIRPLANE, WEATHER

Thermochemistry Thermochemistry is the branch of physical CHEMISTRY that studies the amount of heat gained or lost in a given chemical reaction. It also studies the effect of temperature upon the speed and the direction in which a chemical reaction takes place. Both engineers and scientists need the data obtained about the heat properties of chemical reactions so that they can calculate certain thermodynamic properties of substances.

Modern thermochemical results are now usually reported in terms of the *calorie* rather than in terms of the joule. The calorie is scientifically defined as the amount of heat needed to raise the temperature of one gram of water one degree centigrade. The calorie is related to the amount of mechanical work to which it is equivalent: one calorie of heat equals 4.184 joules of mechanical work.

When a change in state occurs, the heat effects accompanying this change are measured in a calorimeter. The CALORIMETER is a reaction vessel immersed in a tank of water, and isolated from its surroundings. The rise in temperature of the water is measured with a sensitive thermometer. The product of the rise in temperature and the total heat capacity of the water and calorimeter tank is a measure of the heat evolved.

Thermochemical data usually are expressed as follows:

$$C + O_2 = CO_2 + 94{,}000 \text{ calories}$$
solid gas gas

When one mole (12.01 grams) of solid carbon and one mole (32.00 grams) of gaseous oxygen combine to form one mole (44.01 grams) of gaseous carbon dioxide at constant pressure, 94,000 calories of heat are given off.   D. L. D.
SEE ALSO: HEAT OF FUSION, HEAT OF REACTION, HEAT OF VAPORIZATION

Thermocouple (THER-moh-cuh-puhl) A thermocouple is a device having two junctions, which generates a voltage when the junctions are at dif-

A sensitive ammeter will measure the current produced when the thermocouple (an iron wire and a copper wire) is heated in a flame

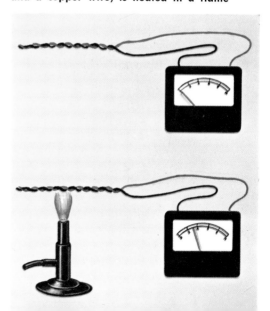

ferent temperatures. Simple thermo-couples can be made by joining any two dissimilar metals, such as iron and copper, at each end. If the two junctions are kept at differing temperatures, a voltage is created, producing a current in the wires between the junctions.

The German scientist, Thomas Seebeck, discovered this thermoelectric effect in 1821 while studying Volta's theory of contact potential between unlike metals. VOLTA knew that this contact effect was much like the voltage produced by a cell using two metals as electrodes; he saw that this potential changed as temperature changed. Seebeck found the voltage change depended only on the temperature of one metal junction, if the other junction were kept at constant temperature. The voltage produced depended on the particular metals used.

The voltage produced by a single thermocouple, even with temperature differences of a hundred degrees, is only a fractional volt. Still, thermocouples are compact instruments. They have many uses.

THERMOPILES

A thermopile uses several thermocouples connected in series to give higher voltages. It is used as a radiation THERMOMETER and high-temperature *pyrometer*. Temperatures inside furnaces are so high that they would melt ordinary mercury-in-glass thermometers. But these temperatures can be found if the radiant heat emitted from the furnace is measured. This can be done by allowing the radiant heat to fall on a thermopile and then measuring the voltage.

As a remote detector, the radiation thermopile is positioned at the focus of a mirror. Astronomers measure the surface temperature of planets by this method, using their telescope mirrors to focus the heat radiation onto one side of a thermopile.

THERMOCOUPLE METERS

Certain alternating currents cannot be measured accurately by an AMMETER. Thermocouple meters are used in which the unknown current heats a wire coil. The heat of this coil is then detected by a junction. The resulting voltage produces a direct current measured by an ammeter.   D. A. B.

SEE ALSO: THERMOELECTRICITY, VOLTMETER

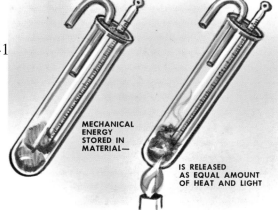

MECHANICAL ENERGY STORED IN MATERIAL—

IS RELEASED AS EQUAL AMOUNT OF HEAT AND LIGHT

The first law of thermodynamics

Thermodynamics Thermodynamics states that energy cannot be destroyed, that energy in other forms tends to be converted to heat energy, and that a pure crystal at absolute zero would have a completely ordered arrangement of atoms.

Thermodynamics is based upon two important relations that have been observed in the interconversion of heat and mechanical, electrical, or other forms of energy. These relations are known as the first and second laws of thermodynamics.

The first law of thermodynamics is also called the *Law of Conservation of Energy*. It may be expressed in several ways: (1) energy may change its form, but it cannot be created or destroyed; (2) when work is transformed into heat, or heat into work, the quantity of work is mechanically equivalent to the quantity of heat; (3) the HEAT entering a system is equal to the increase in energy of the system plus the external work done by the system during the entry.

Heat and motion are both forms of energy. When hot gases in an automobile cylinder push the piston, the gases become cooler. Heat energy is lost, but an equal amount of energy of motion takes place. When objects are rubbed together, energy of motion is lost; but equal heat energy takes its place.

The second law of thermodynamics is often called the *Law of Degradation of Energy*. This law is based on the observation that it is impossible to completely convert a given amount of heat energy into an exact amount of another kind. The reverse process, however, can be carried out. Heat cannot be completely converted to work because some of the work produced is immediately turned back into heat due to friction. To reduce friction, the conversion could be made infinitely slowly. But an infinitely slow

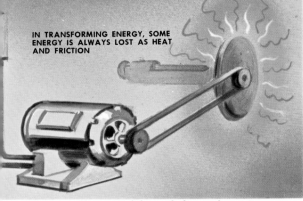

IN TRANSFORMING ENERGY, SOME ENERGY IS ALWAYS LOST AS HEAT AND FRICTION

The second law of thermodynamics

process would require an infinitely long time and therefore would not correspond to any real process.

Since other forms of energy tend to be converted into heat, any system tends to change spontaneously so that this conversion to heat occurs. Also, since the system cannot be put back into its original state except by using extra energy, heat is a more *degraded* form of energy than other forms.

The molecular theory of heat states that heat is the motion, or vibration, of the molecules of a substance. The greater the heat of a substance, the greater the motion of the molecules. This molecular motion is disordered and random. The degraded nature of heat is due to this randomness.

To obtain a measure of the randomness of a system, a quantity called *entropy* is used. For a real system, the increase in entropy is always greater than that for an ideal system.

The second law gives the increase in entropy during a process but it does not give the entropy before the process began. To do this, the third law of thermodynamics is needed. It states that at absolute zero, the entropy of a pure crystal having a perfectly ordered arrangement of molecules would be zero. From the second and third laws, the actual entropy of a substance at any temperature can be calculated.

The laws of thermodynamics explain why perpetual motion machines are impossible. Some energy is always lost in the form of heat and would have to be replaced in order to keep the machine running.

However, the laws are limited to molecular sizes and above. On the atomic level we find that electrons may revolve around the nucleus of an atom indefinitely without friction and without a gain or loss of heat and, if energy is added to the electron system, the electrons absorb only definite amounts.   H. W. M.

SEE ALSO: AUTOMOBILE, ENERGY, ENGINE, MOLECULAR THEORY, MOTION

Thermoelectricity

Thermoelectricity Thermoelectricity is electricity that has been produced by the direct conversion of heat energy into electrical energy.

This can be accomplished because the atoms of elements are able to gain or lose electrons. This ability can be altered by heating the atoms. For example, copper atoms gain electrons more easily than zinc atoms. Zinc atoms lose electrons more easily than copper. If a long strip of zinc and a similar strip of copper are pressed together at both ends to form two junctions, some of the electrons will leave the zinc and go over to the copper. The copper will acquire a small negative charge due to the extra electrons, and the zinc will acquire a slight positive charge due to the loss of electrons. Therefore, any additional loss of electrons by the zinc quickly becomes impossible because of zinc's positive-charge attraction for electrons and copper's negative-charge repulsion of electrons.

In 1821 Thomas Seeback discovered that heat altered the atom's ability to gain or lose electrons. Seeback heated one copper-zinc junction and cooled the other. More electrons were lost by the zinc and gained by the copper at the hot junction than at the cold. The hot end of the copper then had more electrons than the cold end. Since electrons repel one another, some flowed down the copper strip to the cold end. But cold copper can't hold as many electrons as hot copper and some electrons went back to the zinc strip. The resulting thermocouple can generate electric current indefinitely as long as the temperature difference between the junctions is maintained.

In 1834 Jean Peltier discovered that if an outside electrical source was connected to Seeback's thermocouple, one junction would absorb heat while the other junction would radiate heat.

Modern technology uses these discoveries in many ways. A thermocouple made of high melting point wires and connected to a properly calibrated ammeter can measure the high temperatures inside a blast furnace. Since a very small electrical current can be detected, an insulated junction can be aimed at the stars and measure the heat coming to the earth from these bodies. By using hot and cold gases instead of wires, a thermoelectric generator is currently being developed which will generate electricity without moving parts.

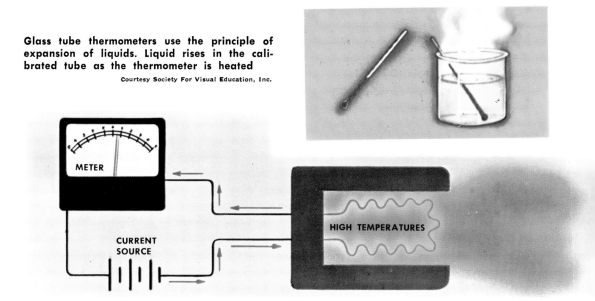

Glass tube thermometers use the principle of expansion of liquids. Liquid rises in the calibrated tube as the thermometer is heated

Courtesy Society For Visual Education, Inc.

METER

CURRENT SOURCE

HIGH TEMPERATURES

Pyrometers are used to measure high temperatures. As the wire becomes hotter, it becomes less able to conduct electric current. A meter measures the current from the wire

Peltier's device is being used in small compact refrigerators.   B.A.T.
SEE ALSO: THERMODYNAMICS

Thermograph see Thermometer

Thermometer A thermometer is an instrument that tells how hot or how cold a thing is; it measures *temperature.* The temperature of the air outside has an effect on what clothing a person wears. Many foods must be cooled to or cooked at certain temperatures. A furnace must heat at the correct temperature to keep a house warm and comfortable. A thermometer of some kind is used to measure all these temperatures.

Man's early thermometers were rather crude devices. The great GALILEO invented one that measured temperature by the expansion and contraction of air. It was undependable, though modern *Beckman air thermometers* are very exact for measuring small ranges of temperature change. The first *alcohol thermometer* was invented in 1641. Gabriel Daniel Fahrenheit, in 1714, perfected glass-tube thermometers filled with mercury. About thirty years later, Anders Celsius devised the CENTIGRADE scale. In modern times, electric thermometers (THERMOCOUPLES) have been developed.

Thermometers have a great many uses. *Clinical* thermometers are used to measure body temperature. Florists use thermometers so they can keep their greenhouses at the proper temperatures. The measurement of temperature is important in the manufacturing of bricks, china, and glass. An automobile utilizes a thermometer gauge to indicate water temperature. Chemists and physicists rely upon accurate thermometers in their experimentation.

The most common type of thermometer is the glass tube, liquid thermometer. It utilizes the principle of liquid expanding in volume when heated, and contracting in volume when cooled. MERCURY is the liquid element in many household and scientific thermometers. Mercury, because of its high boiling point, is employed for reading high temperatures. Alcohol, with its low freezing point, is the liquid used for reading low temperatures. Many of the wall and outdoor thermometers use alcohol, colored blue or red.

Bimetallic thermometers consist of two metals, such as steel and brass, welded together. Brass expands about twice as fast as steel; therefore, the fused metals bend as the temperature climbs. The *thermograph,* or recording thermometer used by the weather bureau, employs a bimetallic element.

The resistance thermometer and the thermoelectric thermometer are both elec-

✳ **THINGS TO DO**

MAKING AN AIR THERMOMETER

1 Locate two empty pill bottles or similar containers. Purchase a one-holed stopper for one of the bottles, or make one by drilling a hole in the center of a cork. It will be necessary to put wax around the hole after a piece of glass tubing has been inserted to make the bottle airtight.
2 Fill the second bottle with colored water. Invert the bottle with the stopper over the second bottle, and immerse the end of the glass tube into the solution.
3 Fasten this apparatus to a wooden support.
4 A scale may be calibrated from the readings of a commercial thermometer. When the temperature drops, does the fluid go up or come down in the tube? Does air expand or contract when it gets colder?

tric devices. The platinum thermoelectric thermometer can measure temperatures to 1500° C. (2732° F.). High-temperature thermometers are called *pyrometers.*

Temperature is measured in units or degrees. The degree is not the same on all thermometers. The three modern scales of temperature are *Fahrenheit, Centigrade (Celsius),* and *Absolute* (Kelvin). P.F.D.

SEE ALSO: ABSOLUTE ZERO, HEAT, TEMPERATURE, TEMPERATURE SCALES, THERMOSTAT

Thermonuclear reaction Thermonuclear reactions occur at very high temperatures. At a temperature of 10 million degrees Kelvin, hydrogen nuclei fuse together to form helium. This reaction produces a tremendous amount of energy. Thermonuclear reactions are the source of energy in the sun and stars. They are being studied as a future energy source. A.J.H.

SEE: NUCLEAR ENERGY

Thermostat A thermostat is an automatic device which regulates temperatures. When a cake is baked in an oven, the thermostat is set for a certain temperature. The oven remains at this same temperature because the thermostat controls the amount of heat entering the oven.

Numerous modern machines and appliances are controlled by the action of thermostats. An automobile's cooling system is regulated by a thermostat which controls the flow of water through the motor. The automobile cigarette lighter is also thermostatically regulated. Home furnaces require a thermostat to keep the temperature at the required number of degrees. Refrigerators, toasters, electric irons, and electric blankets are governed by thermostats. A modern jet airliner requires hundreds of thermostats to help control its complicated engines and instruments.

Thermostats depend upon the expansion and contraction of metals, liquids, or gases. This expansion is used to operate valves or levers or to make or break electrical contacts.

One of the most common thermostats is

Parts of a Thermostat

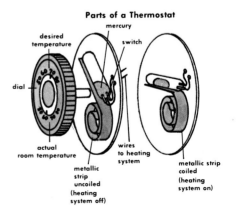

the bimetallic strip thermostat in which two strips of different metals are fused together. These metals expand at different rates when heated. The bimetallic strip bends as it becomes warmer and straightens when cooled. At a certain temperature, the bar closes an electrical contact, making an appliance, furnace, or machine operate.   P. F. D.
SEE ALSO: AUTOMATION, HEAT, TEMPERATURE, THERMOMETER

Thigmotropism see Tropism

Thirst Thirst is the sensation which warns that the body needs water. It occurs when the body is losing more water than it is taking in. *Cellular dehydration* in the brain is thought to trigger the thirst sensation.

Thistle This is a common name for a number of plants. They are weedy HERBS and are pests in gardens, meadows, and grain fields. Both leaves and stems are spiny and prickly. The flowers are shades of purple and blue. Fruit is dry and one-seeded.

The Canadian thistle, a perennial, grows to about 5 feet (1.5 meters) and has silky, fragrant, purple flowers. After the blossoms wither, the flower heads form large, downy seedballs that are scattered by the winds. Sturdy, spreading roots start new plants.

Scotch thistle is a biennial, with lavender blooms, 9 feet (2.7 meters) tall. Globe thistle is a cultivated plant 5 feet (1.5 meters) with blue flowers. Both are in the Compositae family. Russian thistle or "tumbleweed" is in the goosefoot family.   H.J.C.
SEE ALSO: WILD FLOWERS

Thomson, Sir George Paget (1892-1975) Sir George P. Thomson and Clinton Davisson won the 1937 NOBEL PRIZE in physics. Thomson studied the nature of the electron that had first been discovered by his father.

Thomson, a British physicist, established the diffraction characteristics of electrons. Using diffraction methods, his experiments proved the wave-particle theory. His work initiated investigations into surface layers, films, and gases.   A.J.H.

Thorax The thorax is the middle part of an insect's body to which the wings and legs are attached. It is also the part of a vertebrate's trunk, between the neck and the abdomen, containing the heart and lungs.
SEE: INSECTA

Thorium (THOHR-ee-um) Thorium is the 90th element. It is radioactive. Pure thorium is a grayish-white lustrous metal, and can be molded and drawn into fine wires. Thorium and tungsten are in filament wires in light bulbs. It was discovered by Berzelius in 1828.

Thorium can be attacked by concentrated acids, and forms the oxide upon being heated in the air. Salts, such as formate, nitrate, and oxide, are used in medicine. Thorium, with mass number 232, is used in nuclear reactors along with uranium, with mass number 235. The chemical symbol is Th.   M. S.
SEE ALSO: ELEMENTS

Thorn A thorn is a short, modified stem without any leaves. Thorns usually grow out of the bud of a plant.

Honey locust and hawthorns have true thorns. Projections on cacti are modified leaves and should be called spines. The epidermal outgrowths on rose, blackberry, and raspberry bushes are prickles.   H. J. C.

Thorn apple see Hawthorne

True thorns usually arise from the axil of a leaf, or slightly above it

Brown thrasher

Thrasher Thrashers, mockingbirds, and catbirds all belong to the same family. Most of the sixty species of thrashers are tropical American birds. Only eleven species occur north of Mexico.

The common *brown thrasher* is a little larger and thinner than a robin. Its back is a bright, rusty red and its underparts are striped. It is often confused with the THRUSH, but thrashers are larger, have streaked rather than spotted underparts, longer tails, and down-curved bills. Their eyes are yellow rather than black.

Thrashers live in the undergrowth around the edges of forests. They dig into the ground for insects. They sing in the morning and evening from the top branches of the trees, sometimes imitating other birds. Nests are made on the ground of twigs, rootlets, and leaves. Three to six grayish-white eggs, finely speckled, are laid. J. C. K.

Threadworm see Nemathelminthes, Pinworm, Worms

Thrombin see Blood

Thromboplastin see Blood

Thrombosis (thrahm-BOH-siss) Thrombosis is a condition in which a blood clot is formed within a blood vessel or in the heart. The blood clot is called a *thrombus*. When this occurs in the coronary artery, it is a *coronary thrombosis*. A clot may occur when there is a change in the inner coat of a blood vessel. Such a change may be the result of inflammation, tissue injury, or aging.

In order for a blood clot to form, a substance, *fibrin,* must be present. Fibrin is not normally present in the blood. It is the end product of several chemical reactions. Before fibrin is formed, *thrombin* must be present. Thrombin arises by the interaction of *prothrombin, thromboplastin,* and *calcium.* Thrombin interacts with *fibrinogen* to form fibrin. Under the microscope fibrin resembles a threadlike mesh. Blood cells in the blood vessels are trapped in these meshes.

A blood clot may leave the site of its formation, travel through the blood stream, and eventually lodge in a smaller blood vessel. Such blocking of a vessel by a traveling clot is called *embolism.* Those tissues which depend on nourishment from the clogged blood vessels undergo degeneration when the blood flow stops reaching them.

When a coronary thrombosis prevents blood from getting to a portion of heart muscle *(myocardium),* the muscle dies or *infarcts.* Then the person has a myocardial infarction, or *heart attack.* A brain embolism or thrombosis causes a stroke or cerebro-vascular accident (CVA). A *pulmonary* (in the lungs) embolism can be a cause of sudden death. New medications can dissolve embolisms. Blood thinners can help prevent clots from forming, and prevent recurrent strokes or heart attacks.

G.A.D./E.S.S.

SEE ALSO: BLOOD, CIRCULATORY SYSTEMS

Thrush There are several hundred species of thrush throughout the world. The common characteristics of these birds are small, slender bills, strong legs on which they hop, and spotted breasts. The robin and bluebird are thrushes.

The *grayish thrush* is abundant in middle America. It is similar to the robin except for its tan breast. The *wood thrush, veery, hermit, olive-backed,* and *gray-checked thrushes* are shy forest thrushes that breed in North America and winter in South America. They have reddish or greenish-brown backs, and heavily spotted breasts. They eat insects and some worms, spiders and fruit. Their nests are on the ground or in low trees; their eggs are greenish-blue. E.R.B.

Thrust see Aerodynamics

Thulium (THU-lih-um) Thulium, element number 69, is a scarce metallic element in the rare earth group. Compounds of thulium have a characteristic pale green color. It was discovered by P. T. Cleve in 1879.

In nature, thulium (symbol Tm) is found in combination with other rare-earths in minerals such as gadolinite and euxenite. It has very little commercial value except for its stable isotope Tm^{169}. This isotope, when irradiated in a nuclear reactor, forms Tm^{170}, which can be used as a radiation source for portable X-ray equipment as it gives off X-rays. It has atomic weight 168.934. I. K. F.

SEE ALSO: ATOM, ELEMENTS, ISOTOPE

Thunder Thunder is produced by violent expansion of air, which is caused by the tremendous heat of lightning.

Light waves travel about 186,000 miles (300,000 kilometers) per second, while sound waves travel about 1,100 feet (335 meters) per second. Therefore, the sound of thunder is heard after the flash of LIGHTNING is seen.

At times lightning may occur behind a cloud so that the cloud is illuminated. This is called *sheet lightning*. V.V.N.

Thundercloud see Weather

Thunderstorm Thunderstorms are local, relatively small-area storms that are caused by the rapid uplifting of warm, moist air. This forms dark cumulo-nimbus clouds. Associated with thunderstorms are lightning, thunder, short, heavy rain, gusty winds, and often hail.

Individual thunderstorms usually do not last for more than an hour or two, but it is possible for a location to have several thunderstorms at different times on the same day.

Cumulo-nimbus clouds and thunderstorms result when warm, moist air is forced to rise rapidly. This causes condensation to take place and is followed by heavy precipitation. The upward movement of air may be caused in two ways. *Air mass* or local thunderstorms occur within an air mass on warm days when

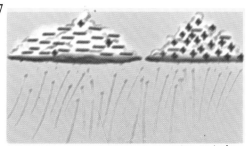

The upward motion of the air against raindrops causes clouds to become charged with static electricity

Earth acquires the opposite charge. A sudden discharge from negative to positive results in lightning

Clouds form as warm moist air meets a cold front

warm, moist air is further heated by the earth's surface and convectional currents develop. This type of thunderstorm is also called a *thermal* or *convectional* thunderstorm.

Frontal or *cold-front thunderstorms* are associated with well-developed cold fronts. They may occur at any time of the day or year. They develop as a rapidly moving cold front forces warm, moist air to rise. This type of storm may develop along the entire front, and the line of the thunderstorm forms what is known as a *squall line*. This may be miles (kilometers) wide and more severe than the local thunderstorm.

Lightning results from the shattering and tearing apart of raindrops within the cumulo-nimbus clouds. Frictional electrical charges are produced which, when the charge becomes strong enough, are discharged as lightning. Lightning can occur within a cloud, between two clouds, or between a cloud and the ground. A lightning "bolt" is really a series of flashes. H. S. G.

SEE ALSO: PRECIPITATION, WEATHER, WEATHER FORECASTING

Thyme, an herb

Thyme (TYME) Thyme is a low, shrubby herb with narrow, tiny leaves on short, hairy stems. It has a bitter, fragrant odor when crushed. In cooking, it is used to flavor soups and dressings.

In drug making, *oil-of-thyme* extract gives flavor to dental preparations. The pure oil, *thymol,* is extracted by steam distillation. The oil was formerly used as a drug to treat hookworm. The plant came from the Mediterranean region where it still grows in a natural state. Ancient people used it as an incense and in cooking.   D. A. B.

Thymus (THY-muhs) The thymus is a pink gland that is located below the neck and behind the top of the breastbone. It is between the lungs and near the heart. Small at birth (weighing about ⅓ ounce or 9 grams), it increases to about the size of a teacup by adolescence. Thereafter, it gradually decreases in size until, in old age, it is quite small.

The thymus is an ENDOCRINE GLAND. It has

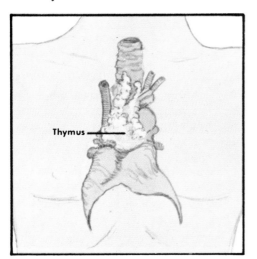

Thymus

no ducts and so secretes directly into the blood. One or more of these glands occurs in all vertebrates but at various locations. In fish they are found along the gill arches; in amphibians, at the jaw angles; in higher reptiles (crocodiles) and birds, they are along the esophagus.

The probable function of the thymus has only recently been discovered. It seems to control body immunity to disease. When the body is invaded by foreign substances (pollen, germs), lymphocytes in the blood make chemicals called antibodies. These combine with the foreign substance, making it ineffective and creating an immunity to that particular substance. Lymphocytes acquire this ability from the thymus. Mice, without the thymus, do not reject skin grafts and have low resistance to disease. Children with abnormal thymuses show similar effects. J. C. K.
SEE ALSO: ENDOCRINE GLANDS, GLANDULAR TISSUE

Thyroid The thyroid is a small gland in the neck below the voice box. A large thyroid which appears as a swelling at the base of the throat is called a simple goiter. The most common kind of goiter is caused by too little iodine in the food.

Near the sea coasts the soil and water contain enough iodine, but far inland, glacial soils lack iodine so that foods grown there contain too little of this element for healthy thyroid growth. Today iodides are added to food salts to prevent simple goiter.

Another and more severe thyroid deficiency in children results in *cretinism,* a condition characterized by dwarfness, puffy skin, and mental retardation. In adults severe deficiency results in *myxedema,* characterized by thick puffy skin, scant dry hair, and mental dullness. Taking thyroid extract helps alleviate these conditions.

Hyperthyroidism, or over-active thyroid, causes nervous excitability, goiter, and protruding eyeballs. Cure is accomplished by removal of part of the thyroid gland by surgery.

The thyroid is an endocrine gland which produces *thyroxin* which regulates general METABOLISM. The rate of production of the thyroid gland is regulated by the *anterior pituitary* gland.

The thyroid gland is deep red, and consists of two lobes joined by a tissue bar, or *isthmus,* stretching across the front of the neck. Each lobe has many microscopic, round, closed sacs filled with a colloid, lined with cuboidal cells, and surrounded with blood vessels and nerves. The thyroid's lymphatic vessels are numerous and large.

The thyroid gland is found in the young lamprey but not in the adult. The shark has a single median thyroid; other fish have a pair. Amphibians have a thyroid that consists of numerous amounts of gland tissue close to the end of the membrane around the heart. In reptiles the thyroid is found close to the windpipe, and in birds the gland is paired and close to the arteries supplying the head. A thyroid with lateral lobes is found in all mammals.   E. M. S.

SEE ALSO: CRETIN, ENDOCRINE GLANDS, EPI-THELIAL TISSUE, PITUITARY GLAND

Thyroxin (thy-RAHK-sihn) see Thyroid

Tibia see Skeleton

Location of the thyroid gland

Tick A tick is a tiny animal that attaches itself to man, birds, and other animals. It lives by sucking their blood. This PARASITE is no bigger than the tip of a nail. It swells up to the size of a thumb as it fills with blood. One meal may last from three to five years. Ticks can carry Rocky Mountain spotted fever or Texas fever from infected animals to humans.

American dog tick

The head, thorax, and abdomen are fused, forming a continuous body. A small part of the head region is hinged to the body to give a movable base to the mouthparts. The tick clings to its host with its strong mouthparts. Larvae have six legs and adults have eight. The tick is an *arachnid.*

Ticks can move to people from dogs or other animals or from grasses and shrubs. Eggs are laid on the ground by thousands. The larvae climb into grass and brush off onto animals. A tick must be pulled out gently or its sucking mouthparts may be left in the host and disease may spread. Alcohol, gasoline or a match will free the head.   C. L. K.

SEE ALSO: ARACHNIDA, METAMORPHOSIS

Tick fever see Animal diseases

Tidal wave The term "tidal wave" is misleading because this type of wave has nothing to do with the tides. It is caused by a disturbance on the ocean floor, such as an EARTHQUAKE or a violent volcanic eruption, or a severe storm at sea. These, in turn, produce a wave or waves that may be over 75 feet (23 meters) high with crests up to a few miles or kilometers apart.

Many oceanographers refer to this type of wave as a *tsunami,* a Japanese term. They are called seismic waves when they are the result of the earth's crustal movement.

In angry seas, a tidal wave is not easily detected, for a ship rises smoothly toward its crest. When it rushes upon land, the crest may become high and powerful, and cause a great amount of damage.   H.S.G.

SEE ALSO: TSUNAMI, WAVE

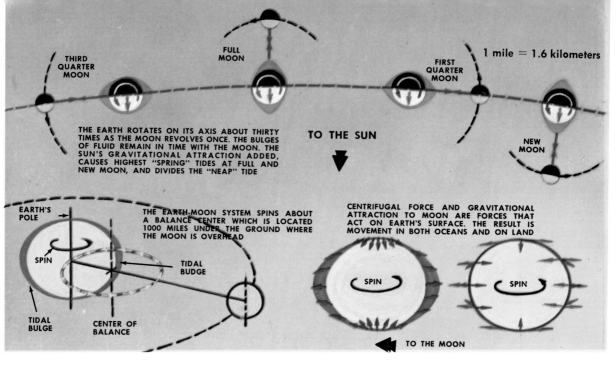

THIRD QUARTER MOON

FULL MOON

FIRST QUARTER MOON

1 mile = 1.6 kilometers

TO THE SUN

NEW MOON

THE EARTH ROTATES ON ITS AXIS ABOUT THIRTY TIMES AS THE MOON REVOLVES ONCE. THE BULGES OF FLUID REMAIN IN TIME WITH THE MOON. THE SUN'S GRAVITATIONAL ATTRACTION ADDED, CAUSES HIGHEST "SPRING" TIDES AT FULL AND NEW MOON, AND DIVIDES THE "NEAP" TIDE

EARTH'S POLE

SPIN

TIDAL BUDGE

TIDAL BULGE

CENTER OF BALANCE

THE EARTH-MOON SYSTEM SPINS ABOUT A BALANCE CENTER WHICH IS LOCATED 1000 MILES UNDER THE GROUND WHERE THE MOON IS OVERHEAD

CENTRIFUGAL FORCE AND GRAVITATIONAL ATTRACTION TO MOON ARE FORCES THAT ACT ON EARTH'S SURFACE. THE RESULT IS MOVEMENT IN BOTH OCEANS AND ON LAND

SPIN

SPIN

TO THE MOON

Tide Tides may be defined as the regular rise and fall of sea level. The main cause of the tide is the gravitational attraction of the moon. On most seacoasts, the tides rise twice to a high point and fall twice to a low point every twenty-four hours. The tide greatly affects water currents, creates and destroys beaches, makes problems for sailing vessels, and affects the breeding habits of many kinds of animals that live in the tidal zones.

Tides are not uniform throughout the world. Some coastlines have very high tides, others quite low ones. In some places, there is only one tide daily, as in the Gulf of Mexico. The height of the tides also varies from 1 or 2 feet (.3 to .6 meter) at Tahiti and Hawaii to over 50 feet (15.2 meters) in Canada's Bay of Fundy. In other places, there are two high tides and only one low. Elsewhere only one high tide separates two lows. A rising tide is said to be *flowing,* and a falling one, *ebbing.*

Causes of tides are numerous and still not fully understood. The chief causes are the MOON and sun. Since the moon is much closer to the earth than the sun, its gravitational pull is more than twice as great as the sun's, although the sun's mass is 27 million times as large! On one side of the globe, the sun or moon, or both, pulls the water toward itself. Because the ground surface of the earth is also pulled, its opposite side is slightly flattened, causing the water to rise from *inertia* so that high tide occurs simultaneously on opposite sides, or *antipodes,* of the earth. The same thing happens when a person is suddenly pulled to one side by one arm. The other arm tends to fly outward and away from the direction of the pull.

When the moon is either full or new, the sun and moon are in a straight line with the earth. Their combined force raises the ocean to its maximum high levels, called *spring tides.* However, when the moon is at an angle from the line from Earth to sun during its first and third quarters, it pulls against the sun. High tides, called *neaps,* do not then run so high.

Another factor causing tides is *oscillation.* Just as a large pan of water will rock back and forth when it is disturbed, so the OCEAN waters also rock in the basins which they occupy. These basins occur throughout the ocean, some covering thousands of square miles, others much fewer. When the tide and the *period,* or *rhythm,* of oscillation coincide, tides are greatly exaggerated.

The shape of the local basin and shoreline also affect tides. Water forced into a narrow channel will undergo a funneling flow, and thus will rise very high on the sides of the channel. This is true in the Bay of Fundy. On the other hand, the island of Tahiti is situated in a very large, open basin; therefore, tidal rise is slight because it is distributed over a very wide area.

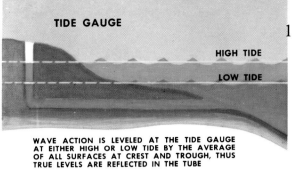

TIDE GAUGE

HIGH TIDE

LOW TIDE

WAVE ACTION IS LEVELED AT THE TIDE GAUGE
AT EITHER HIGH OR LOW TIDE BY THE AVERAGE
OF ALL SURFACES AT CREST AND TROUGH, THUS
TRUE LEVELS ARE REFLECTED IN THE TUBE

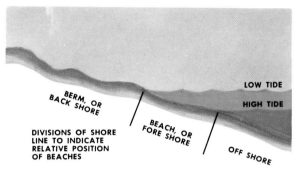

BERM, OR
BACK SHORE

BEACH, OR
FORE SHORE

LOW TIDE

HIGH TIDE

OFF SHORE

DIVISIONS OF SHORE
LINE TO INDICATE
RELATIVE POSITION
OF BEACHES

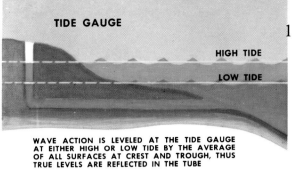

Some rivers that empty into the sea experience *tidal bores*. A tidal bore occurs at high tide when the incoming tide rushes upstream into the mouth of the river. There are many different factors that can cause a river to experience tidal bores. One factor may be the height of the tide itself. The shape and depth of the river mouth may be a factor, as well as the shape and slope of the continental shelf. In some places tidal bores cause rapids in the river. The largest and most dangerous bore occurs in the Tsientang River in China; its crest averages 9 to 10 feet (2.7 to 3 meters). At spring tide it may run as high as 25 feet (7.6 meters).

Tides are important in maintaining beaches. The inter-tidal zones are sandy or graveled stretches of shore line which occur between high and low tidal levels. In general, beaches are built up during the summer by deposits of sand laid down by relatively gentle tides and strong on-shore waves. During stormy seasons, usually in winter, the outgoing or off-shore currents are turbulent and swift; and they carry the sand out to sea.

Beach areas are further divided into three zones. The *berm,* or back shore, is the area of dunes and low mounds which is never wetted by the sea. Below that lies the *foreshore,* or beach proper, this area lies between the highest tidal mark and the lowest ebb. Below the lowest ebb is the *offshore* region, entirely under water.

The term "tide" is often used to describe both "tidal waves" and "riptides." In both cases the terms are misleading because the regular tides of the ocean have nothing to do with them. A TIDAL WAVE is the result of some type of disturbance on the ocean floor such as an earthquake or violent volcano. A tidal wave can also be caused by huge storms at sea. To distinguish it from a true tide, oceanographers refer to a tidal wave as a *tsunami*. A *riptide* is really a swift, offshore current produced by a combination of large breakers and shoreline currents, not directly by the tide.   R. N. J.

SEE ALSO: OCEANOGRAPHY, SEA LEVEL, WAVE

Tiger see Cat family

Tiger lily see Lily

Timber see Economic botany, Forest products, Forestry

Time zones If one were to travel across continents or oceans, one would notice that the time changes in certain places. When traveling from east to west, it is necessary to set a watch back one hour at these certain places. But when traveling from west to east, a watch must be set ahead. These places where time changes are the beginning of new time zones.

Since time changes as the earth spins on its axis from west to east the earth has been divided by man into time zones. Imaginary lines are drawn from the North Pole to the South Pole, much like the dividing sections of a peeled orange. These lines are called lines of *longitude,* or *meridians*.

In 1884, at the Washington Meridian Conference, nations of the world agreed to divide the earth into time zones. These zones were based on lines of longitude or meridians 15 degrees apart. Since 360 divided by 15 equals 24, it is apparent that each time zone marks one hour on a day's time. Approximately one hour passes as the earth rotates for each 15 degrees of its surface. One complete rotation occurs in 24 hours.

The conference also decided that the meridian of the city of Greenwich, England, would be the meridian of 0 degrees longitude. Meridians east of Greenwich up to longitude 180 degrees are called *east* longi-

✳ **THINGS TO DO**

TELLING TIME AROUND THE WORLD

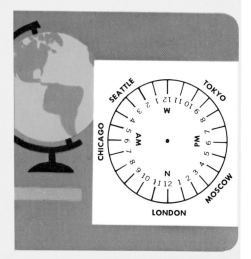

When it is noon in Chicago, what time is it in London or Sydney?

1 Fasten a circle in the center of a large sheet of tagboard with a clip which permits the circle to rotate.

2 Mark off the circle into twenty-four equal parts by bisecting the center. These lines will serve as the longitudes of the earth.

3 Number them consecutively from 12:00 P.M. around to 11:00 A.M. Using a globe find the longitude of a particular city in which you are interested and write it on the corresponding line of your time table.

4 As you work with this instrument you will become very proficient at quickly estimating time around the world.

tude, while all meridians west of Greenwich up to 180 degrees are called *west* longitude.

As an example of time zones, consider Philadelphia, which is 75 degrees west longitude. This is five time meridians west of Greenwich. Therefore, there is a difference of five hours between the clocks of Greenwich and Philadelphia.

"Daylight saving" time is a local adjustment, advancing an hour ahead of the accepted meridian time. This is done to allow an added hour of daylight.   V. V. N.

SEE ALSO: CALENDAR, EARTH, GEOGRAPHY, INTERNATIONAL DATE LINE

Timothy Timothy is a GRASS which comes up year after year (perennial). Its long slender leaves may measure a foot (.3 meter) in length. It has little food value for humans. The name of this grass came from Timothy Hanson, the man who brought it from Europe in the early 1700s.

Timothy, a hay plant, is a forage crop for livestock. Its seeds may be added to lawn mixtures; however, it is not a desirable grass for this purpose.   D.J.I.

SEE ALSO: GRASSES

Tin Tin is a soft, white metallic element. It is highly malleable, which means it can easily be hammered into thin sheets. If a piece of pure tin is bent, it produces a crackling sound. When tin is exposed to low temperatures over a long period, the metal crumbles to a gray powder called *tin pest* or *tin disease.*

The leading ore from which metallic tin is obtained is called *tinstone* or *cassiterite,* formula SnO_2. Most of the world's supply comes from Malaya, Bolivia, and Indonesia. Tin (symbol Sn from Latin *stannum*) has atomic number 50 and atomic weight 118.69.

Since tin ore usually contains many impurities, these must be removed before the metal can be extracted. The ore is roughly pulverized and concentrated by washing and frothing. The ore is then roasted to oxidize impurities such as sulfur and arsenic. Acid-soluble impurities are removed by leaching the ore with acid. The tin oxide is then reduced with carbon:

$$SnO_2 + 2C \rightarrow Sn + 2CO\uparrow$$

As the molten tin, 99.5 per cent pure, flows away from the impurities, it is cast in blocks (block tin).

Tin plate—for the coating of tin cans—is an important product of tin. Thin sheets of iron or copper are dipped into melted tin—a process similar to galvanizing. Tin prevents iron from rusting, but once the tin surface is broken, the iron will rust faster than usual.

Because of its low melting point, tin is a

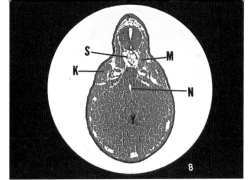

Close up of the section below the head of a frog. M: mesoderm is forming muscle tissue. S: cells will form part of the backbone. K: mesoderm will develop into the kidney. N: gut will enlarge as the surrounding yolk is used up.

leading component in many ALLOYS, such as Wood's metal, Rose's metal, solder, type metal, Babbitt metal for bearings, bronze, bell metal, and pewter. Due to tin's malleability, tin foil was used in the wrapping of candies, gum, and many foodstuffs. The growing scarcity of tin has led to the substitution of aluminum foil, plastics, and papers. Block tin is used in the food industry for moving slightly acidified solutions, such as carbonated beverage syrups. It also is used in water stills.   D.L.D.

SEE ALSO: ELEMENTS, METAL

Tinbergen, Nikolaas (1907-1989) Tinbergen studied the group behavior of animals. He helped us understand why humans are violent. In 1973 he shared a NOBEL PRIZE with KARL VON FRISCH and KONRAD LORENZ.

Tinbergen, Frisch, and Lorenz pioneered the social behavioral science of ETHOLOGY. Tinbergen studied the *relief signals* that animals exchange with their fellows, like courting "dances," territorial calls, and aggressive-surrender rituals.

He criticized society's use of war technology by describing how lower mammals prevent themselves from killing their own kind. Animals relieve their violent feelings with face-to-face signals, such as baring their teeth or "making faces" (especially primates). We humans invent long-range weapons, thus foregoing those natural relief signals that hold back violent behavior.

D.A.B.

Tincture A tincture is an ALCOHOL solution of some drug or medicine. It contains a single element such as iodine, or a single compound, or the part of a plant which will dissolve, such as cinchona bark.

SEE: DRUGS

Tintype see Photography

Tissue see Anatomy, Histology

Tissue culture Animals are made of many thousands of cells. Each cell in the body of a frog, a chick, a mouse, or a human has its own work to do to keep itself alive and to keep the whole animal alive. Each cell also depends upon the rest of the body to supply it with food and to carry away waste materials that poison it. For these reasons, it was believed for many years that cells could not live if they were removed from a living animal.

Many years ago, however, it was learned that cells can live outside the animal's body if they are given a proper place to live in, if they are supplied the right food, and if the wastes can be removed. Keeping cells alive outside the animal's body is called tissue culture.

In 1907, Ross Harrison removed small pieces of very young *embryonic nerve tissue* from the developing egg of a frog and placed them in hanging drop cultures of clotted lymph taken from an adult frog. He carefully sealed them so that they would not be contaminated with bacteria or mold. He found that the nerve cells not only stayed alive, but grew actively and migrated out into the clotted medium. This experiment was the beginning of the tissue culture technique.

Alexis Carrel, a Nobel Prize winner, improved further the methods of keeping cells alive outside the body. Strains of connective tissue cells originally taken from the heart of a developing chick have been kept alive for over 25 years—certainly many times the normal life span of the chick.

In the early days of tissue culture, the juices extracted from embryonic tissue provided the nutrients, and the clotted plasma of adult chicken blood was the preferred growth medium. Strict aseptic conditions were necessary so that bacteria and fungi would not invade the cultures. Today, after years of experience, it has become simpler and more successful to use synthetic materials for a culture medium and antibiotics to control bacteria and fungi.

It is advantageous to isolate cells in a tissue culture to study what these cells can do when they are not under the influence of the rest of the body. It is also possible to watch cells in a tissue culture under the microscope in a living condition. Moving pictures can be taken of their activities. Various kinds of cells have been studied alone in tissue culture: for example, nerve cells, heart cells, kidney cells, cancer cells. By watching these cells grow, it is possible to study how they develop, what makes them assume certain shapes, and what relationships exist between various cells.   B. B. G.
SEE ALSO: HISTOLOGY

Titanium (tye-TAY-nee-um) Titanium is a shiny, white metal element discovered in 1791 by Gregor. Since it was hard to purify until recently, its many uses are just being learned.

Titanium oxide is important for making light-shaded paints because of its white opaqueness. Modern methods for purifying the element have led to its use in many corrosion-resisting, strong ALLOYS. The atomic number of titanium (symbol Ti) is 22, atomic weight 47.90.   D. A. B.
SEE ALSO: ATOM, ELEMENTS

Titmouse A titmouse is a small, fluffy bird. It lives in the woods, eating insects and insect eggs and seeds. It moves like an acrobat around a tree hunting for insects in the bark and leaves. Titmice are closely related to chickadees.

Tufted titmouse, a common forest bird

Many colorful species live in Europe, Asia and Africa. The *tufted titmouse,* a grayish crested bird with brown spots near its legs, lives in the eastern United States. The *plain titmouse* of the Southwest is similar except for the brown. The *bush tit,* a small brownish-gray bird, lives in flocks in the scrubby plants of the West. Titmice nest in holes, which they stuff with leaves and moss. They lay speckled white eggs.   E. R. B.

Titov, Major Gherman Stepanovich (1935-) Titov, a Russian cosmonaut, the first man to spend a day in space, began his journey in his 5-ton (4.5-metric ton) spaceship *Vostok II* on August 6, 1961, at 2 A.M. (EDT). After 17½ orbits (about 436,000 miles or 700,000 kilometers), requiring 25 hours, he returned to earth.

Major Titov was born in the Altai region, Siberia. After completing his secondary education in 1953, Titov trained as a USSR Air Force jet pilot. He then became one of the cosmonaut candidates. In 1962, he joined Colonel John Glenn in the United States to appear before the third International Space Science Symposium sponsored by Space Research.   M.W.C.
SEE ALSO: SPACE TRAVEL

Titration (tye-TRAY-shun) Titration is one of the ways a chemist tests a solution to find out its strength. He uses, for his titration, a solution whose strength he already knows (a standard solution).

In practice, the unknown solution—an acid of unknown strength, for example—is put in a beaker; and the solution of known strength, in this case a base (caustic), is dripped into the beaker from a long tube or *burette.* An indicator, usually a colored organic compound, which has been added to the unknown solution, changes color when just enough base has been added to the solution to neutralize the acid. After the amount of base used in the titration is noted, a calculation can be made to determine the strength of the unknown acid solution. M. S.
SEE ALSO: ACIDS AND BASES, ALKALI

TNT see Explosives

Toad

Toad Toads and FROGS are tailless AMPHIBIANS. While very similar to one another in many ways, there are differences between them. Both breed in water, but toads spend more time on land. Toads have drier, warty skins. Frog skins are smooth and slippery. Toads hop; frogs leap. Toads are both fatter and wider than most frogs and have larger eyes. Frogs and toads are in the same order but different *genera*.

Toads have strong hind legs which enable them to hop about looking for insects to eat. They catch food with their quick, sticky tongues attached at the front of their mouths. Toads have large mouths but no teeth.

The toad has no tail. Its brownish back is covered with lumps and warts. It is grayish-white underneath and speckled with black spots. This coloring helps the toad to hide from its enemies. The toad has short forelegs with separate toes. Its long hind legs have partially webbed toes.

Toads need water in which to lay eggs; hence, in temperate regions breeding usually occurs during the rainy season. Males select the breeding spots and call to the females. Usually, a pond is chosen that will not dry up until the young have hatched. Most toads lay two jelly-like strings containing about 8,000 eggs. They are fertilized as they are laid. Tadpoles hatch in just a few days. During the next two months, the tadpoles grow larger, the long tail is absorbed into the body, legs appear, and lungs replace the gills. The toad then moves to dry land where it may live as long as thirty years.

The toad hibernates in cold weather. It does some of its breathing and much of its drinking through its skin. It sheds and devours its own skin periodically. It spends much of its time half buried in the dirt. When attacked by an enemy, it may puff up its body. Its only efficient means of protection are skin glands which secrete a distasteful acid irritant.

The internal anatomy of frogs and toads is similar. They have a complete DIGESTIVE SYSTEM, with a LIVER and PANCREAS. Excretion is by a KIDNEY (called a *mesonephros*).

Buchsbaum

During the mating season in spring, the shrill call of the male toad to the female can be heard at night near water

Courtesy Society For Visual Education, Inc.

The toad's shrill call is made with the aid of an inflatable air sac in its throat

The toad rolls its long sticky tongue into its mouth when it is not in use

The CIRCULATORY and RESPIRATORY SYSTEMS are like those in the frog. The NERVOUS SYSTEM is typical of VERTEBRATES.

Sex in some male toads can be reversed. Capping the anterior end of the TESTIS is a structure called *Bidder's organ*. If the testis is removed in a young toad, the Bidder's organ develops into an ovary and the young male becomes a functional female.

Toads have worldwide distribution and occur in many types of climates. They are not native to Australia and New Guinea but were introduced into these islands.   J. C. K.

SEE ALSO: AMPHIBIAN, METAMORPHOSIS, PROTECTIVE COLORATION

Toadstool Toadstool is a term sometimes applied to poisonous MUSHROOMS — fleshy, umbrella-shaped fungi. It was once believed that toads sat on them.

Tobacco This herb belongs to the potato or Solanaceae family. It is not dangerous to touch, like poison ivy, but smoking the leaves may affect the proper functioning of the body. An alkaloid nicotine is responsible for tobacco's narcotic property. It is used in some insecticides to kill pests.

In 1964 the Advisory Committee to the Surgeon General of the Public Health Service in Washington did research on the effect of smoking on health, and found evidence that smoking is a hazard. Current legislation requires manufacturers to print a health warning on each package and in all advertising and has banned cigarette advertisements on television.

Despite warnings, people continue to smoke. The world production of tobacco totals over 12 billion pounds or 5½ billion kilograms.

Tobacco, originally an American tropical plant, has been adapted for cultivation in subtropical and temperate climates. It is an unbranched annual, with large oval leaves.

The tiny tobacco seeds are planted in seed beds, and the seedlings are transplanted when they are 4 to 6 inches (10.2 to 15.2 centimeters) tall. The best soil is a light, sandy loam, rich in humus and well fertilized. Tobacco requires careful cultivation. When it is fully ripe, as indicated by a change in the color of the leaves, either the plant, or its leaves alone, are cut.

The freshly harvested leaves are allowed to wilt and then are hung upside down in "curing" barns. Freshly cured leaves must be sorted and aged before using.   M.R.L.

SEE ALSO: NICOTINE

Todd, Sir Alexander R. (1907-) In 1957 the NOBEL PRIZE in chemistry was awarded to Sir Alexander Todd, who studied nucleic acids, which are very important in living things.

Todd contributed to biological and organic chemistry. He was one of the first to study the structure and synthesis of thiamine, vitamin B_1. He also studied vitamins B_{12} and E. His work demonstrated the potential of the HEMP plant as a base for several narcotics. Todd researched the components of the cell nucleus, which contains nucleic acids. These acids can be broken down into *purine* and *pyrimidine* compounds. Todd determined their structures—an important factor in the study of HEREDITY (genetics).   A.J.H.

Tomato The tomato is an herb of the nightshade family. The fruit is a *true berry* filled with many small seeds. Man uses the fruit as a vegetable. The perfect flowers have parts divisible by five. The fruits were once called "love apples." The tomato plant is native to Central America.

The plant looks like a small bush with tiny yellow flowers. As the tomatoes grow heavy, the branches bend to the ground unless they are tied to a stake. The plant should be started in a warm greenhouse and then transplanted to sunny ground. The leaves have a strong scent and are rough .

The fruit of the tomato plant is usually green until it ripens to a bright red. Some kinds of tomatoes are white or yellow when ripe. There are many varieties of tomato plants developed to grow under different conditions.   P. G. B.

SEE ALSO: VEGETABLE

Tongue (TUNG) The human tongue is a thick, muscular organ in the mouth. TASTE buds, important to the sense of taste, are found on it. The tongue helps in chewing and swallowing food. It is necessary for speech.

All vertebrates have tongues. The tongue of a FROG or a TOAD is sticky. It is attached at the front of the mouth and can be flipped out quickly to catch prey. In fish, the tongue projects up from the floor of the mouth, and is neither muscular nor freely movable. Among snakes, the tongue is probably an organ of smell (olfactory recep-

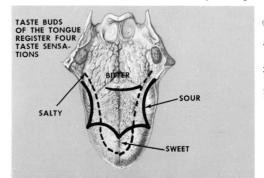

TASTE BUDS OF THE TONGUE REGISTER FOUR TASTE SENSATIONS

BITTER

SOUR

SALTY

SWEET

©Denoyer-Geppert Co.

tor). When inside the mouth, it is retracted into a sheath. The bird tongue lacks well-developed muscles, and is usually covered by horny material.   M. R. L.
SEE ALSO: DIGESTIVE SYSTEM, VOICE

Tonsillitis (tahn-suh-LYE-tiss) Tonsillitis is infection of the tonsils, very common in children and adults. The tonsils become red and swollen; swallowing becomes painful. As a rule, fever and severe pain develop.

Although most cases of tonsillitis are caused by viruses, those caused by streptococcal bacteria must be treated with penicillin to avoid the rare complications of RHEUMATIC FEVER and/or NEPHRITIS.

A *culture* of germs from a swabbed throat is grown in an incubator to see if *beta hemolytic strep, group A* develops. G.A.D./E.S.S.

Tonsils Tonsils are lymphatic tissue in the nasal passage and the throat. These glands filter out and destroy bacteria which may have entered the lymph vessels.

Tonsil tissue is divided into three groups: they are the *lingual* tonsils on the back of the tongue, the *pharyngeal* tonsils, or adenoids, in the nasal passage, and the *palatine* tonsils on either side of the soft palate. The palatine tonsils are the largest mass. It is the palatine section that sometimes becomes chronically infected, requiring surgical removal.   J. C. K.
SEE ALSO: LYMPHATIC SYSTEM

Tonus see Muscle system

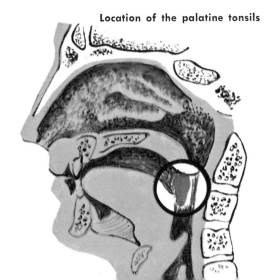

Location of the palatine tonsils

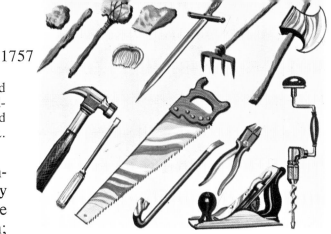

Tools The history of man's development is revealed in the nature of his tools. The very first tools were simple objects of nature. Man's own fists and feet were striking tools. His nails and teeth helped him cut. His hands were tools for holding and shaping. His arms, legs, and jaws could supply leverage for moving.

Sticks and stones, the first tools other than the body, were used in many ways. By lashing a stick to a stone, man made a hammer that was effective for striking. By smoothing and sharpening the edge of a flat stone, a knife was made which had a more durable cutting surface than the jagged edge of a shell or the splinter of hard wood.

Gradually, man also discovered the uses for metals. Thus from the Wood and Stone Age, man progressed into the Bronze Age. He made files and crude tongs during this period. After he discovered iron and ushered in the Iron Age, man developed new tools which were stronger and longer-lasting than those invented earlier. As the variety and quality of tools increased, civilization also developed.

STEEL was an important discovery in the Middle Ages, but was principally used for weapons. During the 1700's, steel tools were made. Later, alloy steel was developed, and led to the manufacture of hard, flexible

HORIZONTAL MILLING MACHINE

PLANING MACHINE

AUTOMATIC GUIDING MACHINE

LARGE RADIAL DRILL

tools that were stronger, sharper, and more durable than any ever known before. Later in the 1700's, tools were designed that could be driven by mechanical power; thus the Machine Age began.

Today there are tools of every imaginable kind. There are striking tools (hammers), cutting tools (saws), shaping tools (lathes), holding tools (vises), leverage tools (crowbars); and there are grinding tools, boring tools, measuring tools, guiding tools, and many special-purpose tools that are used by specialized tradesmen, such as the jeweler, gardener-farmer, bricklayer, and so on.

Many hand tools make use of four of the six simple machines; the *lever,* the *wedge,* the *inclined plane,* and the *screw.* The other two principles of simple machines —the *wheel and axle,* and the *pulley*—are used in complicated machine tools.

HAND TOOLS

While the principles of hand tools have changed little throughout the centuries, the shape of many have changed considerably.

The hammer, with its many variations, is a striking tool. It is also used to crush. The screwdriver is actually a leverage tool, although its main use is to tighten or to loosen screws. Both the hammer and screwdriver are general-purpose tools.

In the cutting and shaping category are the saw, the chisel, and the plane. Saws cut material in many different ways, depending upon the type of saw. The wood chisel chips wooden surfaces if the handle end is hammered. The cold chisel does similar work to metal surfaces. The plane cuts and shapes wood surfaces.

The bit, brace and reamer are drilling and reaming tools. The bit and brace is a standard drilling tool, while the reamer enlarges a hole to a more accurate diameter.

Measuring tools come in many varieties, including the folding rule, the metal tape rule, many gauges, micrometers, calipers, combination squares, and compasses.

MACHINE TOOLS

A machine tool is a power-driven tool that alters the size, shape, or finish of material such as metal, wood, or plastic. A true machine tool does at least four chores. It holds a workpiece, holds a cutting tool, moves one or both of these objects, and provides a feeding movement for the tool or the workpiece. The machine tool performs with exceptional precision and accuracy. It is therefore possible to produce two parts, or thousands of parts, that are identical.

Machine tools may be small bench devices or complicated machines weighing hundreds of tons. They produce tiny nuts as well as huge turbine rotors, both with precision. A machine tool may perform thousands of operations, often directed by a computerized *Numerical Control System.* The various tasks of these tools can be summarized in terms of seven basic operations: *turning, milling, planing, drilling, sawing, grinding,* and *metalworking.*

The lathe is a basic tool for the turning operation. By rotating a workpiece against a fixed tool, the tool produces a cylindrical surface. A milling machine is used to produce a flat, curved, or irregular surface. Unlike the lathe, the milling machine feeds the workpiece against rotating cutters. In the planing operation, a planer or shaper produces a flat surface. Drill presses make holes, while borers or boring mills enlarge or perfect the holes (reamers accomplish the same task faster). A tapping machine threads the inside of the hole.

A variety of power saws, including circular, band, and reciprocating saws, are used to cut metal and wood. More recently, the use of LASER beams and high temperature *plasma-arc torches* has revolutionized the cutting of very hard workpieces. Modern cutting tools have also been made out of hardened ceramic materials, and out of formed and coated powdered metals.

Grinding removes material by feeding a workpiece against a rotating ABRASIVE. Lapping corrects minor surface imperfections. Honers are fine grinders used after boring or reaming. Sometimes, surfaces are perfected by blasting them with streams of sand or other loose media.

Metal-working operations refer to processes which shape metals by pressure, heat, or both. They also include cutting operations. Shears cut the metal, while press brakes, forming rolls, and roll straighteners bend the metal. Hot forging is done on drop hammers and hydraulic presses. The punch press can punch a hole in sheet metal; or when fitted with certain dies, it can punch out the metal following the form of the die pattern.

Many recent advances in machine tools have created ways of cutting and shaping metal without using metal tools. In addition to lasers, high-temperature torches, and special composite cutting tools, negatively charged electric sparks, ultrasound, and high-speed jets of water and other fluids are recently developed methods for cutting and finishing metal.   D.L.D./J.H.

SEE ALSO: ARCHEOLOGY; EVOLUTION OF MAN; MACHINERY; MACHINES, SIMPLE

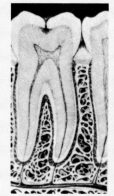
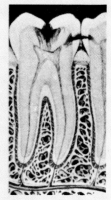

TODAY'S HEALTH, published by AMERICAN MEDICAL ASSOCIATION

In the first stages of decay, the enamel is penetrated. Next, the softer dentine is attacked. Notice how decay affects the neighboring tooth

Tooth decay Tooth decay, or *dental caries,* is said to be mankind's most common disease. It is caused directly by acid made from sugars and starches, by germs or bacteria that live on the surface of the teeth. The more one eats sugar and starch the more acid is formed in the mouth. The acid then may eat through the enamel of a tooth, causing a *cavity* or hole and then decay. If the cavity is not promptly cleaned out and filled by the dentist, the ivorylike dentine or body of the tooth becomes decayed, and eventually the pulp is exposed.

The pulp is killed and an abscess forms. Finally, the molar is extracted and a nearby bicuspid also becomes abscessed

TODAY'S HEALTH, published by AMERICAN MEDICAL ASSOCIATION

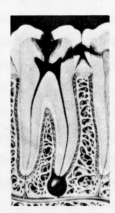

If the exposed pulp is infected, an abscess may occur. An abscess is a pus sac formed at the root-end of the tooth. INFECTION from this spot may be carried throughout the body; so the infected tooth usually must be removed to protect the person's health.

The amount of sugar and starch in the diet does not alone determine the amount of decay that occurs. Some people have teeth which are more resistant or susceptible to decay than others. The condition of the teeth is a factor; a weak condition of the enamel will encourage decay; the acidity of saliva affects decay; and some think a person's emotional state may assist decay.

If food becomes lodged in crevices of a tooth or between teeth and is not removed quickly, these food particles furnish protected breeding places for acid-producing bacteria. The most common decay spots are the spots most difficult to brush—the chewing surfaces of the back teeth, and places where teeth touch each other.

Prevention of tooth decay is still not totally understood. Cutting down on sweets, especially between meals, is recommended to reduce cavities. A healthy, well-balanced diet, regular and proper brushing, and a visit to the dentist at frequent intervals aid in reducing decay. Applying *sodium fluoride* solution to children's teeth (to harden the enamel) helps the teeth resist decay. Some communities now add fluorides to their water supply for this purpose.   D. L. D.
SEE ALSO: TEETH

Topaz (TOH-pazz) Topaz is a valuable GEM (mineral) named after an island in the Red Sea, Topazion, where the gems were once found. Large crystals of blue and white topaz are common all over the world, but yellow topaz is the most valuable because it is the most rare. The finest yellow crystals are found in Brazil.

Uncut natural topaz
J. Daniel Willems

Heat will change yellow topaz to pink. Pink stones are also used in jewelry. Colorless topaz, which has little value, is sometimes cut to imitate diamonds. Quartz may be mistaken for topaz, but true topaz can be distinguished by its greater hardness. Its hardness is 8; its chemical formula is $Al_2(SiO_4)(OH, F)_2$.   J.M.C.

Topography (tuh-PAHG-ruh-fee) Topography is the shape of the land surfaces of the earth. The topography of a region may be shown by a topographic map. Such a map shows the *relief* and the *physical features* of the region. The physical features include plains, hills, valleys, mountains, plateaus, lakes, rivers, and numerous other features. Relief is the difference in height between the highest and lowest parts of the region.

The topography of the earth can be shown on maps in many ways. Color shading is a common means of showing relief. Another method makes use of *contour lines* and produces very accurate SURVEYING of the region. The elevations are plotted on a map and then contour lines are drawn. Every point on a single contour line is at the same elevation above sea level. Much of the surveying needed for topographic maps is done by aerial photography.

Another type of map used to show relief is the three-dimensional, raised relief map.   H. S. G.
SEE ALSO: GEOGRAPHY, MAP MAKING

Topsoil A vertical section through a well-developed soil shows three distinct layers. The fairly loose, porous, usually dark top layer is the *topsoil*. Below this is the lighter more compact layer called the *subsoil*. Below this is the *parent material* from which the subsoil and topsoil is derived.

Topsoil contains sand, silt, and clay and is rich in *humus,* the organic material from decayed plants and animal wastes. Its soluble minerals help plants grow. The bacteria and earthworms in it help fertilize it and keep it porous.   V. V. N.
SEE ALSO: AGRICULTURE, SOIL TYPES

Tornado Tornadoes are the smallest, but most violent of all storms. They vary in diameter from a few hundred feet or meters to a mile (1.6 kilometers). The tornado, a dark, funnel-shaped cloud, travels southwest to northeast at 30 to 40 miles (48 to 64 kilometers) an hour. A tornado may cause extreme destruction.

Tornadoes are small, extremely low pressure areas. They are associated with frontal thunderstorms and squall lines generated when a current of cold air meets a current of warm, moist air. They are often referred to as *twisters* because of the turning motion within the tornado. They occur almost exclusively in the central part of the United States. A tornado that occurs over water is called a *waterspout.* H. S. G.

SEE ALSO: CLOUD, WEATHER

Torque (TAWRK) When a body is acted upon by a force that tends to produce rotation of the body, the result is called the *moment of force,* or *torque.* The value of torque is equal to the force itself multiplied by the perpendicular distance from the line of action of the force to the axis of rotation. This distance is often called the *lever arm* of the force, and the line around which the body rotates is known as the *axis of rotation.*

As an example, consider opening or closing a door. The axis of rotation is the line passing through the hinges. Now, if one pushes against the knob, the force causes the door to rotate on its hinges. Thus, the force must have created a torque. If one pushes on the door at a point closer to the hinges than the knob, a greater force is required than before because the length of the lever arm has been decreased. The distance from force to hinge is less than from knob to hinge.

Now suppose that a bar is pivoted at its center. If a force is exerted on one end of the bar and an equal but opposite force is exerted on the other end, the result will be a turning of the bar. This combination of forces is called a *couple.* A couple is properly defined as a pair of equal forces acting

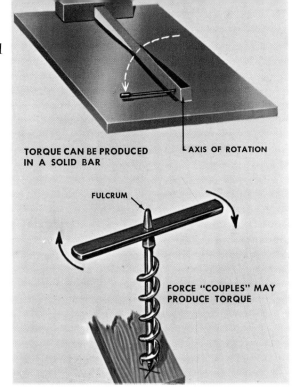

TORQUE CAN BE PRODUCED IN A SOLID BAR   AXIS OF ROTATION

FULCRUM

FORCE "COUPLES" MAY PRODUCE TORQUE

in opposite but parallel lines. The torque produced by the couple will be F times l, where "l" is the perpendicular distance between the forces. Its value will be the same regardless of where the fulcrum is placed.

To simplify the mathematical treatment of torques, a rule known as the *torque rule* is used. It is stated as follows: the sum of the torques acting on any point of a body must be zero (cancel each other out) if the body is to remain in rotational equilibrium. The torque tending to turn a body in a counter-clockwise direction is called a *positive* torque, and the clockwise rotation is called a *negative* torque. It is also true that the sum of the positive torques must be equal to the sum of the negative torques if the body is not to rotate. A. E. L.

SEE ALSO: FOOT-POUND; MACHINES, SIMPLE; TORSION; WORK

Torricelli, Evangelista see Barometer

Torsion (TAWR-shun) The STRESS required to twist a solid body, such as a metal rod or a wire, is called torsion. Rotating shafts in machines (or parts of structures which undergo stress of this sort) must be tested so that the shaft will not be placed under too much TORQUE (force which tends to twist the shaft).

Tortoise see Turtle

Helen J. Challand
Touch-me-not is valued for its bright flowers

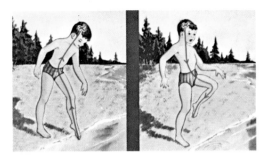

Reaction to cold water involves both the tactile organs and heat receptors

Touch Touch is the sense which enables animals to feel pressure or motion of a solid, liquid, or gas (air movements). The sense of touch can also recognize variation of temperature or differences in such characteristics or objects as shape, texture, or size. All people have this sense, but in some it is better developed than in others.

Stimuli are received by special organs, known as *tactile corpuscles,* which are found in the skin. These organs are sensitive to changes in pressure. They send impulses along nerves to the central NERVOUS SYSTEM which, in turn, causes a muscular reaction or other response, by sending impulses to muscles controlling the part.

Tactile corpuscles are found in greater numbers in the finger tips and the tip of the tongue than elsewhere in the body. The upper back is so thinly provided with tactile corpuscles that certain areas can be touched with a fine point and not be felt. The sensitivity of an area depends upon the number of corpuscles present. Blind persons, or those using the sense of touch in occupations, develop this sense more than the average person. Blocking of impulses by anesthesia, or cutting nerves, eliminates this sense.   D. J. I.

Touch-me-not This name is given to several flowering plants. Some grow wild; others are easily grown in gardens. The name comes from the fact that when ripe pods are touched, they shoot out seeds. These plants belong in the *garden balsam* family.

Impatiens or *jewelweed* is a wild variety of touch-me-not. This bushy plant has a watery stem, alternate leaves, and five-petaled yellow flowers. *Sultana* is also called touch-me-not. It is 15 inches (38 centimeters) tall with reddish flowers.   H.J.C.

Tourmaline Tourmaline is a very complex silicate and occurs in several crystalline forms. The crystals are found in a variety of colors; black and brown are the most common. The tourmaline used for GEMS may be green, blue, deep red, pink, or black.

Tourmaline is a compound of silica, boron, aluminum, and water; it often also contains iron, magnesium, sodium, or lithium, and occasionally fluorine. Tourmaline has a hardness of 7 to 7.5 on the Mohs HARDNESS SCALE. The crystals are generally brittle, although gem tourmaline is less so than the other types. Crystals are used in pressure gauges because they exhibit the PIEZOELECTRIC EFFECT.   D. A. B.
SEE ALSO: MINERALS

Tourniquet see First aid

Toxin see Poison, Vaccine

Tracer see Nuclear science glossary

Trachea see Respiratory system

Tourmaline crystal with the two minerals albite and lepidolite, from California

J. Daniel Willems

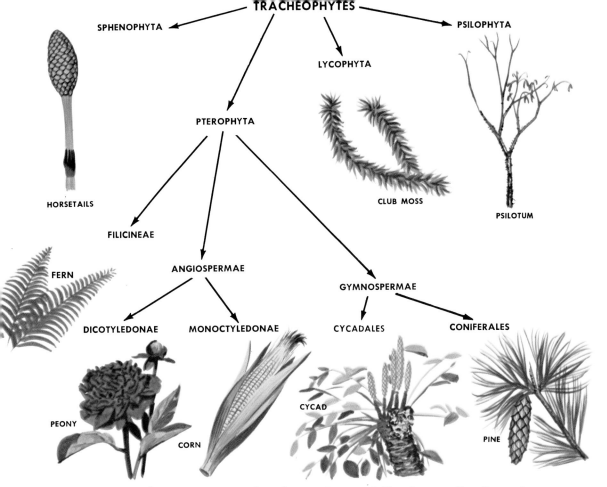

TRACHEOPHYTES

SPHENOPHYTA — LYCOPHYTA — PSILOPHYTA

HORSETAILS

PTEROPHYTA

CLUB MOSS

PSILOTUM

FILICINEAE

FERN

ANGIOSPERMAE

GYMNOSPERMAE

DICOTYLEDONAE — MONOCTYLEDONAE — CYCADALES — CONIFERALES

PEONY

CORN

CYCAD

PINE

Tracheophytes (TRAY-kee-oh-fytes) This is the highest division in the plant kingdom. The plants in this division are true land plants with protective tissues or secretions or both on their surfaces. Most have roots for anchoring, erect stems, and fairly large leaves. All have special conducting tubes called *tracheids*. There are over 240,000 species of tracheophytes, making them the dominant plants in the world. It is believed they evolved from ancient green algae. There are four subdivisions.

Psilophyta: This is the most primitive group. There are only two living *genera;* the rest are fossils. Living members are only a few centimeters high, without roots, and sometimes without leaves. They possess both an underground and an erect stem. The erect stem is green and manufactures foods for the plant.

Lycophyta: This subdivision is composed of small herbs, such as club moss and *Selaginella.* They have roots, stems, and tiny, scalelike leaves. Fossil species were huge trees. Many of these extinct members had true seeds, but the present ones do not.

Sphenophyta: There are 25 living species of this subdivision. They are herbs commonly called horsetails or scouring rushes. Their hollow, aerial stems are jointed; leaves are quite small and wedge-shaped. Fossil sphenopsids were treelike plants.

Pterophyta: This subdivision is the largest and most important economically. Over two thirds of all plants belong in this group. They have roots, stems, and generally large leaves. *Filicinae* is the only class that does not produce seeds. Fossil forms, however, had seeds. Members in this class include adder's-tongue, grape ferns, and true ferns. Class *Gymnospermae* produces naked seeds borne on cone scales. They lack flowers and fruits. This group consists of cycads, ginkgos, and conifers. Finally, class *Angiospermae* includes all the flowering plants. This is the only group that has vessels in stems made of XYLEM cells for conduction of raw materials. Class *Angiospermae* is divided into two subclasses—the monocotyledons and the dicotyledons. H.J.C.

SEE ALSO: PLANTS, CLASSIFICATION OF

Trade winds Trade winds are steady, strong winds that blow across the Atlantic and Pacific oceans. In the Northern Hemisphere, they blow from the northeast toward the southwest; in the Southern Hemisphere, from the southeast toward the northwest. These winds have a definite path, from about 30° N. latitude to about 30° S. latitude, which shifts slightly with the seasons. They are called trade winds because their paths marked trade routes in the days of sailing ships.

At the equator, air is constantly heated; it rises vertically and then moves toward the poles. This warm, rising air creates a belt of low pressure at the equator known as the *doldrums* or a belt of calms.

As this air rises into higher altitudes, it is cooled, and it descends at about 30° N. and 30° S. latitudes. This descending air creates belts of high pressure called the *horse latitudes*. Since the air here is moving in a vertical direction, this is also a belt of calms.

As this descending air nears the surface of the earth, it starts to move horizontally as wind, part moving away from the equator and part toward the equator. That part moving toward the equator becomes the trade wind belts. In the Northern Hemisphere, deflected to their right by the earth's rotation, they become the *northeast trades*. In the Southern Hemisphere they are deflected to their left and become the *southeast trades*.

The trade wind belts shift north and south with the seasonal shifting of the sun's vertical rays. *Hooked trade winds* develop when the doldrum belt is entirely north or south of the equator. As the trades cross the equator, they receive a deflection to their original hemisphere and so become *hooked*. This is important to places near the equator since it means they will have different prevailing winds during a year.   H. S. G.
SEE ALSO: HEAT, WEATHER, WIND

Trailing arbutus (ahr-BYOO-tuhs) Trailing arbutus, or *mayflower,* is an evergreen plant that is related to azaleas, rhododendrons, and laurels. This slightly woody perennial spreads along the ground. It has very fragrant pink or white flowers that grow in thick clusters.

The thick leaves are pointed or blunt at the tip, and heart-shaped or rounded near the stem. The fleshy, almost round, fruit splits open at maturity.

Trailing arbutus grows in rocky or sandy soil in the woods of Canada, and as far south as Florida.   D. C. H.

Train, railroad The railroad train consists of a locomotive which moves attached passenger or freight cars over fixed rails. The basic purpose of this vehicle is to transport people and materials in large volume at little cost.

Railroad trains were first constructed in the United States about 1826, but at this time they were horse-drawn vehicles. In the early 1830s, the steam locomotive was developed as a self-powered mover. In a little over one hundred years, the railroad train became a fast, quiet, smokeless, and comfortable means of transportation.

Great flexibility of rail car movement has been accomplished by the adoption of a standard gauge, or width, of 4 feet 8½ inches (143.5 centimeters) between rails. When railroads were first built, as many as 23 different gauges were used. Now, trains can travel from Canada to Mexico without hindrance by odd-gauged tracks.

RAILROAD LOCOMOTIVES

The locomotive is a power plant on wheels, designed to pull or push a number of railroad cars. The dominant source of power used by locomotives is the diesel engine. This internal combustion engine uses petroleum as a fuel. Electrical engines are also used in a limited number of locations.

The steam-engine-propelled locomotives, which were the first type used, have been replaced by diesel locomotives only within the past 40 years. The diesel locomotive is far more efficient than the steam engine; it produces more horsepower and weighs less. The diesel engine can go

Left, aerial view of railroad yard at Corwith. Below, left, Super Chief near Flagstaff, Arizona. Below, right, coaxial train—train of the future—capable of carrying passengers and freight at high speeds

(All, Santa Fe Railway)

farther without fuel stops. Also, it does not have to take on water. Diesel engines have fewer maintenance problems, spend less time being serviced, and are far more economical to operate.

The characteristics required for the locomotive depend upon its use. For example, passenger locomotives are designed for pulling relatively light loads with fast acceleration and at high speeds.

Freight locomotives pull heavier loads, with slower acceleration and speeds, than passenger locomotives. To increase the power required to pull a train, several locomotives are often coupled together to operate as one unit. A freight locomotive pulling 100 cars and weighing 7,000 tons (6,350 metric tons) requires a pulling capacity of 21,000 pounds (93,351 newtons) on level track once the train has reached a steady speed. For each 1 percent rise (grade) in the track, the locomotive must pull an additional load of 140,000 pounds (63,500 kilograms). Similarly, curves offer a resistance of about .5 pound (2.2 newtons) per ton (.91 metric ton) of load hauled for each degree of curvature. To accelerate this train one mile per hour, each second would require an added pull of 700,000 pounds; to accelerate the train one kilometer per hour, an added pull of 5,000,-000 newtons would be needed. For these reasons, grades (slopes) are kept below 2 percent and tracks are laid as straight as possible.

RAILROAD CARS

Railroad cars convey either passengers or freight. Passenger cars include (1) coaches, which seat from 50 to 80 people in long-distance travel and up to 170 in double-deck commuter coaches; (2) sleeping cars with varying types of room arrangements; (3) dining cars, which are restaurants on wheels; and (4) lounge and observation cars for rest and relaxation. Baggage and mail cars are usually included as part of the passenger train.

Tank cars are cylindrical tanks that haul many types of liquids. Perhaps the most familiar car is the caboose, attached to the end of the freight train. It serves as the train crew's headquarters, and its cupola provides a view of the train's operation.

DECLINE OF PASSENGER TRAFFIC

Railroad passenger traffic has declined drastically with the increase in airplane and automobile travel. However, with newer trains and better service, travel by trains is becoming more and more popular.　　H.P.O.

SEE ALSO: ENGINES, MOMENTUM

Trajectory see Astronautics

Tranquilizer A tranquilizer is a DRUG that calms excitement and tension. Tranquilizers are useful in treatment of mental distress.

Chlorpromazine (Thorazine) was one of the first drugs given to severely disturbed patients. Newer drugs of the benzodiazapine class (Diazepam or Valium) are often used to treat simpler forms of anxiety. Overdosage can cause depression of respiration. ADDICTION to tranquilizers is rare, but dependence does occur.

Transformer A transformer is a device for increasing or decreasing the voltage in an AC electrical circuit. For example, a transformer is used to lower the voltage supplied at the wall outlet to a voltage suitable for operating model trains or other electrical toys.

A transformer consists of two separate, insulated coils of copper wire, wound upon a magnetic steel frame, or *core.* The first coil, or *primary winding,* is connected to the source of current to be altered in voltage. The current within the primary coil alter-

nately magnetizes the core in opposite directions. This constantly changing *magnetic field,* when passing through a secondary coil, or winding, induces a voltage in the secondary by the law of electromagnetic induction. A transformer cannot be used in a DC system, since electro-magnetic induction depends upon a constantly changing current.

The voltage induced in the secondary winding is equal to the voltage of the primary times the ratio of the number of turns on the secondary to the number of turns on the primary winding. When the secondary has more turns than the primary, the voltage induced in the secondary is greater than that of the source, and the transformer is a *step-up* transformer. When there are fewer turns on the secondary, a lower voltage is induced and the transformer is a *step-down* transformer. A step-up transformer steps up the voltage, but not the total energy because watts equal volts times amperes; and amperes are reduced when volts are increased.

Transformers are important in the communications and power industries.   C. F. R.
SEE ALSO: ELECTRICITY, ELECTROMAGNET

Transfusion (trans-FEW-zhun) Transfusion is the transferring of BLOOD or PLASMA from one living creature into the body of another. The person giving the blood is called the *donor.* The person receiving it is the *recipient.* There are four main types of blood: A, B, AB, and O. The donor's blood must be compatible with the recipient's or death may result.

Bleeding from a cut artery or vein can cause rapid loss of blood and SHOCK; replace-

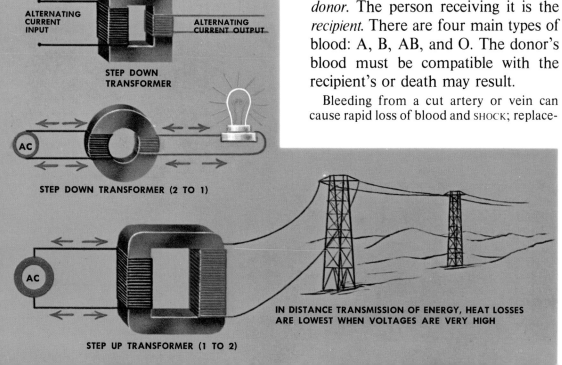

IRON CORE

ALTERNATING CURRENT INPUT

ALTERNATING CURRENT OUTPUT

STEP DOWN TRANSFORMER

AC

STEP DOWN TRANSFORMER (2 TO 1)

AC

IN DISTANCE TRANSMISSION OF ENERGY, HEAT LOSSES ARE LOWEST WHEN VOLTAGES ARE VERY HIGH

STEP UP TRANSFORMER (1 TO 2)

ment of blood by transfusion is necessary. Transfusion must also be given when the bone marrow becomes exhausted and cannot make blood cells.

To perform a transfusion, a pint (.5 liter) of blood is drawn from a vein in the arm of a healthy donor. The blood is carefully *typed* against the recipient's blood. The four blood types and the Rh factor in the blood determine compatibility. Only certain combinations are compatible. Type O can be mixed with all other types. However, O can only accept O blood in transfusion. Type AB can accept any other type but can give to no other type but AB. Types A and B are compatible with only themselves or type O. Any other mixtures will cause the blood cells to clump together or break up *(hemolyze)*. Such a transfusion reaction can be fatal. When the bloods are matched, the donor's blood is injected into a vein of the recipient. In practice, blood from donors is "cross-matched"; so O is given to O, and AB receives only AB.

Only human blood can be transfused into a human. Animal blood is incompatible. Blood taken from a person recently deceased is perfectly good for transfusion.

If the blood is not needed immediately, it can be refrigerated and kept in a blood bank for 30 to 60 days. Blood-borne diseases, such as SYPHILIS, MALARIA, and certain viruses, can be transmitted by transfusion. HEPATITIS is, unfortunately, a complication of transfusion. Some kinds of hepatitis antigens can now be discovered by tests, which decreases the risk of receiving contaminated blood. Since it has been noted that blood from people who sell it causes hepatitis much more frequently than donated blood, all blood must be labeled either "paid for" or "donated." If a surgical operation is not an emergency, the safest way to replace blood is to remove a pint of blood from the patient, refrigerate it, and then transfuse it at the time of surgery.

When there has been no loss of red blood cells, PLASMA alone may be given to replace the loss of fluid. Plasma need not be typed. Other fluids put into the vein are salt, sugar, water, concentrated albumin, white blood cells, dextran, and factors for blood clotting needed to combat HEMOPHILIA.

Tranfusion of large amounts of blood *(exchange* transfusion) is done in babies born with Rh complications. B.M.H.

SEE ALSO: BLOOD TYPES, RH FACTOR

DIAGRAM SHOWING GENERAL CONSTRUCTION OF JUNCTION TRANSISTORS

Transistor (tran-ZISST-er) The transistor is one of the devices which make it possible for a small amount of electrical energy to control a much greater amount. Transistors are made of specially prepared silicon, germanium, or other *semiconductors.* (A semiconductor is a substance which offers less resistance to electric current flow than an insulator but more resistance than a conductor.) When the proper voltages are applied to a transistor, electric charges *already present* within the semiconductor are moved, creating a current flow.

The *junction* transistor is the most important form in present use. It is made as a "sandwich" of two different alloys of germanium, n-germanium and p-germanium. The thin "filler" of the sandwich, the base of the transistor, is made of one material and is sandwiched between slices of the other material. Junction transistors may be either n-p-n or p-n-p transistors; each type offers advantages in certain applications. The electric current in n-germanium is electron flow. In p-germanium, however, the electric current consists of the travel of positively-charged regions, called *holes,* which exist only in semiconductors. The entire transistor is a single crystal of germanium with the proper *impurities* added to make the "sandwich."

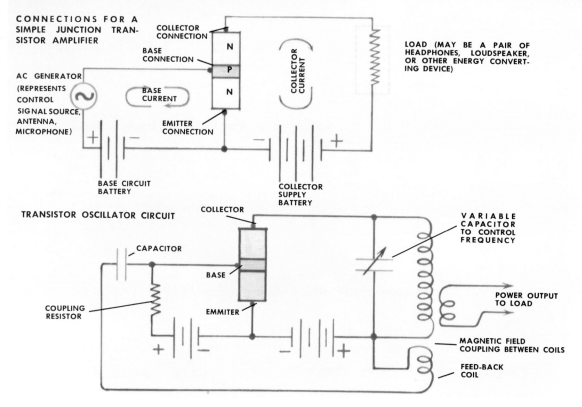

CONNECTIONS FOR A SIMPLE JUNCTION TRANSISTOR AMPLIFIER

COLLECTOR CONNECTION

BASE CONNECTION

N

P

N

COLLECTOR CURRENT

LOAD (MAY BE A PAIR OF HEADPHONES, LOUDSPEAKER, OR OTHER ENERGY CONVERTING DEVICE)

AC GENERATOR (REPRESENTS CONTROL SIGNAL SOURCE, ANTENNA, MICROPHONE)

BASE CURRENT

EMITTER CONNECTION

BASE CIRCUIT BATTERY

COLLECTOR SUPPLY BATTERY

TRANSISTOR OSCILLATOR CIRCUIT

COLLECTOR

CAPACITOR

BASE

COUPLING RESISTOR

EMMITER

VARIABLE CAPACITOR TO CONTROL FREQUENCY

POWER OUTPUT TO LOAD

MAGNETIC FIELD COUPLING BETWEEN COILS

FEED-BACK COIL

To simplify the description, an n-p-n transistor will be described. The p-n-p transistor connected in a circuit operates similarly. The battery connections are reversed when a p-n-p transistor is used. When the base circuit battery is correctly adjusted, only a limited amount of current can flow from emitter to the collector terminals through the transistor and thus through the load. When the AC generator (representing a signal source) makes the base region more positive, more current flows from the emitter to the collector, and then through the load. When the base is made more negative, the collector and load current decreases.

Since the changes in the emitter-collector current may be from ten to one hundred times greater than the changes in the base current which caused them, the transistor is a powerful *signal amplifier,* or *step-up* device. Thus one transistor can amplify the power of an AC signal as much as one hundred times. When even greater amplification is needed, several transistors can be operated in a cascade pattern (one after another).

The circuit just described is called the *common-base* circuit since the base is common to both input and output circuits. A transistor can also be connected with the collector common to both input and output circuits (common collector circuit) or with the emitter common to both circuits (common emitter circuit). The choice of one circuit arrangement over another is usually dictated by what is desired.

If a transistor amplifier is connected so that some of the amplified signal is fed back into the input circuit in the proper phase, the amplifier will become an oscillator. An oscillator is a circuit that converts DC into AC, usually at a frequency much greater than could possibly be developed by an ordinary electromechanical generator. Oscillators are used to generate electrical signals in RADIO, TELEVISION, and RADAR circuits.

Transistors are also used as high-speed switching devices in computers and in telephone central offices. The switching ability of a transistor is one of its most important characteristics.

Because of improved manufacturing techniques, the transistor is not only more readily available but also more reliable. New types appear almost daily, avoiding difficulties formerly connected with its use. New semiconductors, such as gallium arsenide, show promise for sturdier types. It now appears that the transistor, or some close relative of it, may soon replace the vacuum tube completely in most home and industrial devices. Its chief value lies in its long life and small size.   C. F. R.

SEE ALSO: ELECTRICITY, ELECTRONICS, PHOTOELECTRICITY

Translucent Translucent describes a material which diffuses or spreads rays of LIGHT which pass through it. Light can pass through it but objects cannot be seen clearly through it. It is only partly transparent.

Transmission see Automobile

Transmutation of elements This process changes one element into another. It occurs in natural radioactivity. Scientists can accomplish transmutation by bombarding an element with high-speed particles generated by NUCLEAR REACTORS.

SEE ALSO: ALCHEMY, NUCLEAR ENERGY, NUCLEAR SCIENCE.

Transonic see Supersonic

Transparent Transparent is a term commonly used to describe a material which lets the visible rays of the spectrum through it in such a way that the material can be seen through. Other materials are transparent to other kinds of radiation, such as ultraviolet rays.

SEE: LIGHT

Transpiration (trans-pih-RAY-shun) Man gives off water through his skin. This process is called *perspiration*. Plants give off water through their leaves in a similar process called *transpiration*. On a hot day a person can lose 2 pints (.9 liter) of water by perspiration. A single corn plant transpires 2 quarts (1.9 liters) a day. A redwood tree transpires gallons (liters) of water daily.

The minerals in the soil must be dissolved in water before they can enter the root cells. A plant must take in much more water than it needs to get enough minerals to make food. Since the plant cannot hold all this water, it lets the water out through little holes in the leaves.

The roots are continually absorbing water through their root hairs. This water

✳ THINGS TO DO

DO PLANTS GIVE OFF WATER?

1 Tie a clear plastic bag over the leaves and stem of a plant. Be sure none of the plant touches the bag except where it is tied securely around the stem just above the soil level.
2 Set it in the sun for several hours.
3 Observe what happens in the bag. Where does the water come from?

forms columns in the tubes and vessels from the roots to the leaves. Many of the cells in the leaf are next to air spaces. These spaces open to the outside through minute holes called stomata pores. Each is surrounded by two cells (*guard* cells) which control the opening and closing of the pore. As water leaves the cells, it exerts a pull on the water behind it. This transpirational pull is exerted from one cell to another and helps this long column of water to be pulled upward from the roots to the leaves. A plant uses only about 10 per cent of the water absorbed. The excess water is transpired. An acre (.4 hectare) of corn will lose 8,000 gallons (30,300 liters) in a single day. A corn plant needs 500 pounds (225 kilograms) of water to make one pound (.5 kilogram) of plant. Alfalfa needs 900 pounds (400 kilograms), while the cactus needs only 40 pounds (18 kilograms) of water to make one pound (.5 kilogram) of cactus.

Several factors affect the rate of transpiration. Larger leaves, thin cuticle on leaves, greater number of stomata per square inch, low humidity in the surrounding air, strong wind currents, higher temperature, bright sunny weather, and lower air pressure increase transpiration. If the roots do not absorb at the same rate as transpiration occurs, the balance is upset. This causes dehydration or wilting because of the loss of *turgor* in the plant cells.   H.J.C.

SEE ALSO: PLANT, STOMATA

Transplanting Just as a child gets too big for his clothes, so does a plant outgrow the size of the pot in which it is living. A plant may need to be moved or transplanted to a larger pot to let its roots spread out. Plants planted inside need to be moved outside and planted in the garden when the weather is warmer. Transplanting, then, means to move a plant from one area to another or from one container to another.

Transplanting may destroy part of the root system and upset the balance between ABSORPTION and TRANSPIRATION. The plant continues to lose water through the leaves and there is less root surface to absorb the moisture needed. To remedy this, keep the newly transplanted specimen in a shaded area, reduce the temperature, and water it frequently.   H. J. C.

Transplant (organ) A person can be injured and lose an arm or leg or an ear or eye and still live a normal life. These organs are wonderful to have, but they are not needed (*vital*) for the body to live. However, the HEART, KIDNEYS, LUNGS, and LIVER, are necessary to sustain life. If these organs become injured by INFECTION or by hardening of the arteries (ARTERIOSCLEROSIS) they can no longer work and the body will die.

In 1700, blood was first transfused from one human to another. This was the first successful transplant. In recent years many thousands of transplants have been successful. In 1930 the cornea of the eye was transplanted to replace the scarred cornea of a blind man, making it possible for him to see. Many people donate their eyes to eye banks when they die. The eyes can be kept frozen until they are needed to replace an opaque cornea.

For many years skin has been taken from one part of the body and transplanted to cover a badly burned or scarred area elsewhere on the body. Blood vessels grow into the grafted skin and it continues to live. The area from which the transplant was taken heals by forming new skin. Such transplants are called *autografts*. They are nourished by the same blood type and tissue type.

Thousands of kidneys have been transplanted into people whose kidneys have been injured by disease and who would have died from kidney failure. These kidneys have been donated by persons who were dying of causes other than kidney disease and wanted to help someone live.

In 1967 Dr. Christiaan N. Barnard transplanted the first human heart into another man who was dying of heart failure. Since then hundreds of such operations have been performed.

An organ which is transplanted from one person to another is called a *homograft*. An organ transplanted from an animal, such as a chimpanzee or a pig, to a person is called a *xenograft*.

Between 1963 and 1984, animal organs, most from chimpanzees, were transplanted into nearly thirty human patients throughout the world. None of the patients lived for extended periods with the cross-species transplants. In 1984, an infant nicknamed Baby Fae was given the heart of a baboon. She died 21 days after the operation, and no additional xenografts were made until 1992. Several attempts to transplant animal livers into humans ended unsuccessfully in 1992. By early 1993, no successful xenograft had been made anywhere in the world. Today, doctors believe that the future of cross-species transplants may lie in keeping a patient alive until a human organ donor can be found.

The success rate for homografts is much higher, although tissue rejection is often a problem. In August 1992, Chicago scientists reported development of a genetically engineered PROTEIN, CTLA4Ig, which, in animal studies, greatly simplified treatment for tissue rejection. About 16,000 organ transplants were performed in the U.S. in 1992.
                    B.M.H./J.H.

SEE ALSO: IMMUNITY, SURGERY

Transuranium elements The transuranium elements, all in the actinide series, range from NEPTUNIUM, element 93, to element 103. They resemble the rare earths. They are produced by bombarding the atoms of other elements, and are radioactive.

SEE: ELEMENTS

Tree of heaven The tree of heaven is the common name for the *ailanthus* tree. It has long, compound leaves with many long, thin, pointed leaflets. It looks like an overgrown fern. It can grow rapidly and strongly even from a little bit of poor soil near a sidewalk in a city.

The ailanthus blooms in June. Its flowers are thin sprays of small, yellowish blossoms. Some trees produce male, pollen-bearing blossoms and others produce the female, seed-bearing flowers. If the leaves or the staminate flowers are crushed, they give off a strong, disagreeable odor. The pollen flowers fall off, but the seed flowers mature into large, brilliant bunches of seeds. Where a leaf falls from the tree, the branch is left with a gray scar that is shaped like a shield.   C. L. K.

Tree-ring dating is a method of determining the age of a tree. It is the common name for the science of *dendrochronology.*

A tree adds one growth layer per year to its *circumference.* The spacing of these rings or layers reflects periods of both slow and fast growth. These rates correspond to the tree's particular climatic conditions. Tree-ring studies have given scientists clues to the past climates of the earth.   P.P.S.
SEE ALSO: ARCHEOLOGY

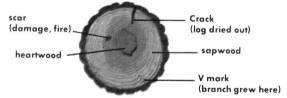

scar (damage, fire) — heartwood — Crack (log dried out) — sapwood — V mark (branch grew here)

Trench, deep-ocean A deep-ocean trench is a canyon-like depression on the ocean floor. Many trenches are found in the oceans, but most are near *island-arcs* and continental margins.

Trenches form as the result of PLATE TECTONICS. They occur as a moving oceanic plate collides with a more stationary plate. The moving plate is deflected downward as the two meet, and gradually sinks into the earth's mantle. As the oceanic plate sinks down, it tends to drag a portion of the crust with it. This creates deep-ocean trenches.

Trenches are the deepest part of the oceans. The Mariana Trench off the Mariana Islands is 36,198 feet (11,033 meters) deep, according to echo soundings.   P.P.S.
SEE ALSO: CONTINENTAL DRIFT

Trench mouth Trench mouth, or *Vincent's angina,* is a disease of the mouth in which the gums, the lining of the cheeks, and the floor of the mouth become dark red, swollen, and sore. It is called "trench mouth" because during World War I soldiers in the trenches had the disease. It is caused by several kinds of bacteria.

Triangle see Geometry

Triassic see Mesozoic Era, Geologic time table

Trichina (trih-KYE-nuh) Trichinae are slender roundworms which may be found in hogs, bears, rats, and humans. The larvae of these small worms are parasites, which means they cannot live freely in nature. The worms pass from one animal to another in pork or bear meat which has not been well-cooked. The young, which are produced in the intestine, make their way to various muscles where they coil up and harden. Only prolonged heat will kill the worms in muscle tissue.

Adult worms are encysted in the muscles of pork and enter a person's disgestive tract when undercooked pork is eaten. The worms lay hundreds of eggs in the intestines. As the larvae develop they begin to migrate throughout the body. They bore through the wall of the human intestine and enter the blood and lymph vessels. They leave these structures looking like perforated sieves in their journey to the muscles. The larvae usually end up in the muscles of the rib, tongue, eye, and diaphragm. They remain there, grow into adults, and die unless this muscle is eaten by another animal.

An animal with trichina worms is said to have *trichinosis.* Since the worms are microscopic, it is impossible for the United States

Governmental agencies to inspect the meat for contamination. The only safeguard against the *Trichinella* worm is thorough cooking of pork.   H. J. C.
SEE ALSO: NEMATHELMINTHES, PARASITES

Trichinosis see Trichina

Trichocyst A trichocyst is a tiny capsule containing a hair-like stinging organ. It is found in some protozoans, such as the PARAMECIUM.

Trigonometry see Mathematics

Trillium see Wild flowers

Trilobite (TRY-luh-byte) Trilobites were a large group of animals that lived in the ocean. They are now extinct. For thousands of years there were probably more trilobites than any other animal in the ocean. Then the other animals that were better adapted came along. The little trilobites began to disappear.

The name "trilobite" means "having three lobes." Their bodies were covered from head to tail by three sections of a shell made of CHITIN—a hard, nonliving substance. Trilobites rolled up in their shells for protection. Most were only 1 or 2 inches (2.5 or 5 centimeters) long. Some, though, got to be over a foot (.3 meter) long. All lived either on the ocean floor or burrowed into the sand.

Trilobites were among the first members of Phylum *Arthropoda*—the group including crayfish, lobsters, and insects. During the Paleozoic Era there were about 1,000 genera and 2,000 species. One of the main differences among them was the size and placement of a *suture,* or slit, in the head end of the chitin. When the animal started molting, the first crack in the chitin was from this suture. After molting, the animal grew a new shell.

Many kinds of trilobite fossils have been found. Because they are so numerous and

from such a definite period, they are often used as *index fossils* for dating Cambrian and other Paleozoic rocks.   J.F.B.
SEE ALSO: EVOLUTION, GEOLOGIC TIME TABLE, PALEONTOLOGY

Triplets see Multiple births

Tritium see Hydrogen

Tropical climate see Climate

Tropical fish The tropics are the very warm lands and waters near the equator. Many kinds of fish live in the warm water. These fish, which are called tropical fish, are beautiful in shape and color. They are so pretty that many people like to collect them and keep them at home in aquariums.

Tropical fish are either marine fish, which means they live in the ocean in salty water, or fresh-water fish, which usually means they live in rivers, streams, and ponds. A marine fish cannot live in fresh water, and a fresh-water fish cannot live in salty, ocean water.

Like most plants and animals that live in the tropics, tropical fish are found in almost endless variety. Colorful reds, silvers, blues, greens, purples—even blacks and glowing fluorescents which sparkle at night —almost every color imaginable can be found in the tropical-fish world. There are the stately, slow-moving angel fish, the speed-demon striped zebras, the friendly kissing gouramis, the ferocious piranhas, the aggressive barbs—gentle, family-loving fish-parents and destructive bullies. The habits of fish are as different and as interesting as the habits of people.

Tropical fish are divided into four groups by their mating habits: the egg-layers, the live-bearers, the bubble-nest builders, and the cichlids.

Egg-layers drop eggs, which later hatch into young fish, in the water. This group includes many beautiful and unusual fish. The butterfly fish has large pectoral fins which allow it to soar out of the water as a "flying fish." The hatchet fish has a bulging belly which is paper-thin when viewed from the front. The blind cave fish and the fierce piranha belong to this group. The

SOME COMMON TROPICAL FISH

1—ANGEL FISH
2—NEON TETRAS
3—TROPICAL CATFISH
4—SIAMESE FIGHTING FISH
5—PLATY, OR MOON FISH
6—FISH HAVE NO EARS. THEY HEAR WITH THEIR BODIES TAKING VIBRATION FROM THE WATER
7—FEMALE SWORDTAIL
8—BLOODFINS

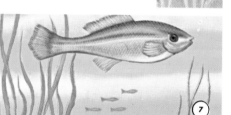

bloodfins; the sparkling, colorful tetras; the glowing rasboras; and the playful barbs are among the most popular of tropical fish. The eel-like knife fish and loaches are interesting additions to the aquarium, as are the bottom-feeding, whiskered catfish, and especially the leopard-spotted corydoras.

The *live-bearers* hatch their eggs inside the body of the female. The young are released as free-swimming babies. This group includes many aquarium favorites: the tiny irridescent guppies; the beautiful mollies which have large, sail-like dorsal fins; the attractive platys of varied colors; and the arresting swordtail with its brilliant color and long, streaming anal fin. In this group of fish, the males are the spectacular specimens, while the females are less showy.

It is fascinating to watch the *bubble-nest builders*. These fish have air-breathing organs, and normally take bubbles of air into their mouths. At breeding time, the male makes a cradle of sudsy air bubbles on the surface of the water. After mating, the male picks up each egg in its mouth, forms an air bubble around it, and delivers it to the floating nest. It is also the father who tends the nest and guards the young after they

hatch. The mother is driven into a corner in submission. The magnificent paradise fish, Siamese fighting fish (betta), and gouramis are members of this group.

The *cichlids* have a highly organized mating behavior. During courtship, the male and female interlock by the jaws into a struggling embrace. If they both outlast this athletic contest, they mate. The eggs are laid in a carefully prepared nesting spot. Then both parents participate in transferring the eggs, a few at a time, from one depression to another that has been prepared in the sand. Some of these fish are mouth-breeders and keep the entire brood in their mouths for as long as 15 days until they have all hatched. It is believed that this mouth care is a kind of "baby bath" which frees the eggs of fungus, a dangerous scourge. The angel fish, the jewel fish, the pompadour fish, and the Egyptian mouth-breeder are some of the better-known cichlids. B. B. G.

SEE ALSO: AQUARIUM, GOLDFISH, GUPPY

Tropical plants see Plants, tropical

Tropics see Cancer (constellation), Capricornus, Earth

Sunflowers exhibit tropism when they turn toward the sun.

✳ THINGS TO DO

IN WHICH DIRECTION DO ROOTS GROW?

1 Put a layer of cotton on a piece of glass. Place several seeds in a row across the center of the cotton. Corn, bean, and radish seeds will germinate quickly.
2 Put a second piece of glass over the seeds and cotton, thus making a sandwich.
3 Tie the glass together, and set it on end in a dish of water.
4 In two or three days the small seedlings will appear. In which direction are the roots growing?
5 After the first week turn the glass sandwich around so the top edge is immersed in the water. Notice the roots are pointing up and the little shoot downward. After a week in this position which part of the plant is growing down toward the center of the earth?

Tropism (TRO-pizm) Tropism is the turning of a plant toward or away from something. Plants lean toward the light. Roots grow toward water. Most stems grow away from the earth. On a sunny, summer day some plants will fold up their leaves. These movements by plants help them get the materials they need to live. They are not able to run around like most animals to get food or get away from things that endanger their lives.

The word tropism comes from the Greek word *tropos,* which means to turn. Parts of different plants may react differently to the same outside stimulus. For example, roots grow toward the earth's center which is positive *geotropism.* A prefix in front of the word *tropic* indicates the outside stimulus to which the plant will react. *Phototropic* means the response to light, *hydrotropic* to water, *chemotropic* to chemicals, *thermotropic* to changes in temperature, *thigmotropic* to touch, and *electrotropic* to current. This irritability toward things in its environment enables a plant to secure the needed raw materials and energy for survival. It is also a safety mechanism to avoid injury. Some leaves will curl up in bright sunlight to slow down the rate of water loss in TRANSPIRATION. Roots will grow away from copper sewer pipes. *Traumatotropism* is the ability to grow scar tissue over a wound to prevent any foreign material from entering.

Tropisms can be explained by understanding the action of a plant hormone *auxin* on plant cells. This hormone controls the growth and other physiological activities. Auxin increases the rate of cell growth. A house plant set in a window receives more light on one side, but the other side is shaded. Since light inhibits the action of auxin, the cells on the side of the plant away from the direct sun grow faster. This causes the plant to lean toward the source of light. H. J. C.
SEE ALSO: PLANT

Troposphere see Atmosphere

Trout A trout is a food and game fish. It is usually found in cold, fresh water in lakes and streams, but a few species live in the ocean. There are more than thirty species in American waters. They eat insects, worms, minnows and other small fish.

Trout often interbreed, so color and marking variations are common. This has given rise to so many local variations that it has become difficult to separate them into species. In addition, some trout, like the steelhead, are silvery when in the sea but show the rainbow pattern when in fresh water. Coloration (red, orange, yellow) is usually restricted to males.

Trout have long, fine-scaled bodies, scaleless heads, and two soft-rayed dorsal or back fins. The fighting trout is a favorite game fish, especially in the United States, where government hatcheries keep streams abundantly supplied. One of the handsomest and gamest trout is the *rainbow* trout, usually found in the rushing streams of the western states. M.R.L.

Chicago Natural History Museum
Lake trout (top) and brook trout

Tsunami (tsoo-NAH-me) Tsunami a Japanese term, is used to describe a seismic sea wave—which is often incorrectly called a TIDAL WAVE.

A tsunami occurs when an earthquake takes place under the ocean. The "shock waves" generated by the earthquake cause the development of these giant sea waves. Tsunamis are not very dangerous in the open ocean, but they are dangerous as they approach the shore or pass through shallow water. P.P.S.

SEE ALSO: EARTHQUAKES, OCEANS

Tuber Tuber is a swollen part at the end of an underground STEM of a plant. The tuber holds the food for the plant. The POTATO is a tuber.

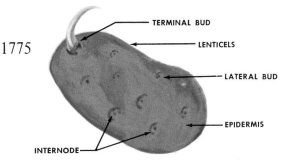

The potato, a tuber, illustrates how all stems, whether above or below ground, are similar to each other in structure

All of the plant but the tuber usually dies when winter comes. The tuber lies dormant until spring when it sprouts at the *nodes,* where the buds or eyes develop. *Internodes* are the spaces between the eyes. The young shoots reach above the ground to form new plants and obtain food from the tuber until their own roots and leaves are formed.

The eyes of the potato appear in a spiral pattern that circles the tuber. Tubers of other plants do not necessarily sprout in a definite pattern. Each eye consists of a ridge holding a tiny, scale-like leaf and usually three buds. Potatoes are usually propagated by planting a piece of potato with one or more eyes.

The tuber is scarred where it breaks from the *apex,* or tip, of the underground stem. This is sometimes called the *rhizome* of the plant. P. G. B.

Tuberculosis (two-BUR-kew-LOW-sis)

Tuberculosis (TB) is a disease caused by a BACTERIUM (*Mycobacterium tuberculosis*). The lungs are most often affected. However, joints, kidneys, and the brain may also be involved. The disease causes fever and loss of weight. Tuberculosis of the lung may cause a cough. Coughing sprays, containing the bacteria, can infect another person who inhales the sputum.

The tubercle bacteria can be inhaled into the lungs or swallowed in contaminated milk or food. In America, contracting TB by inhalation is more frequent than by ingestion. No matter how the bacteria enter the body, they propagate to form a collection of cells called *tubercles.* The bacteria *sensitize* the body so that the skin reacts to an injection of *tuberculin.* A positive skin test means the body contains tubercle bacteria, but it does not mean there is active disease. The bacteria attempt to grow and spread through the body.

The body resists by killing the bacteria or by forming a capsule around them. A constant battle goes on between body resistance and growth of the bacteria. In 99 percent of exposures, no tuberculosis develops. If resistance is lowered by some other illness, stress, or poor nutrition, the bacteria may overcome body resistance and spread, causing tuberculosis. Cavities may form in the lungs, spread to the brain, and cause MENINGITIS.

STREPTOMYCIN and aminosalicylic acid have been used to treat TB. Isoniazid (INH and Rifampin) are more commonly used. People whose skin test "converts" from negative (no reaction) to positive (red, raised lump) are often given INH for one year to help them fight off the disease. BCG vaccine (Bacillus Calmette-Guerin) gives weakened live germs to young people who have a high risk of contracting TB. (They can still get TB, however.) A study of Chicago inner city children who were vaccinated with BCG before age one seems to show that the vaccine may also protect them from some cancers and leukemias.

B.M.H./E.S.S.

Tuberose (TOOB-rohs) The French use Mexican tuberose to make perfume. It is grown in the United States as a garden plant. The fragrant flowers are waxy and white, and appear in the fall. The plant grows to 2 or 3 feet (.6 or .9 meter).

Tuberoses depend upon an underground stem, a *tuber,* to propagate themselves. This structure stores up food for the next year. Usually the productive life is about five years. It is necessary to dig up the tubers before the first killing frost and store them until spring.

D.C.H.

Tuberous begonia see Begonia
Tufted titmouse see Titmouse

Tulips have attractive blue-green foliage
F. A. Blashfield

Tularemia see Animal diseases

Tulip The brightly colored tulip is one of the first flowers to bloom in the spring. The flower and long leaves grow from a bulb or underground stem. Each spring for several years the bulb produces one beautiful flower. Tulips bloom in almost every color from white to a blue so dark that it looks black. Some are streaked with other colors.

While there are over sixty species and countless varieties of cultivated tulips, there are no known wild species of this garden plant.

Since tulips belong to the *lily* family, they have six stamens and one compound pistil originating from several leaflike parts (*carpels*). Tulip leaves seem to grow directly from the ground since none of the plant stem is above the ground.

The word *tulip* comes from the Persian word for *turban.* The plant was grown extensively in Turkey, coming to Vienna, Austria, from Constantinople in the 1500's. Today most of the bulbs are produced in the Netherlands.

J. C. K.

Courtesy Society For Visual Education, Inc.
Single tulips

Tulip tree The tulip tree, also called *yellow poplar,* is in the *magnolia* family. It is an ancient tree, fossil leaves dating back sixty million years having been found in Greenland and Europe. The leaves are squared-off at the ends and deeply notched. Its yellow-green flowers resemble tulips.

The tulip tree, with its large flowers, pointed leaves, and cone-shaped fruits, is an unusual and beautiful ornamental tree

The wood of the tulip tree is soft and can be easily milled or worked. Enormous amounts are used for plywood, boxes, crates, insulation material, and paper for books. A heart stimulant is derived from its bitter inner bark.

The tulip tree grows in the eastern states west to Wisconsin and south to Louisiana and Florida.   D. C. H.

Tumblebug see Scarabs

Tumbleweed

Tumbleweed is a name given to at least two plants commonly found in the midwestern and western prairies, plains, and deserts. These plants may grow to be 2 feet (.6 meter) tall. When the plants are dead and dry in the autumn, they snap off easily near the ground. Since their foliage is round at the top, the plants are easily blown or tumbled about.

Tumbleweeds sometimes collect in masses and resemble great loosely constructed balls of grass blowing along. They are easily caught in fences or along buildings and may be a nuisance. Plants called tumbleweeds include the *Russian thistle* and one of the *amaranths*.   D. J. I.

Tumbleweed, of the amaranth family

Tumor

(TOO-mer)   Tumor means a swelling. It is a growth on or in the body that is not normal. A tumor may occur in any tissue or in any organ of the body. It may be as small as a pea or larger than a grapefruit.

Malignant tumors, such as CANCER, are composed of abnormal cells which divide and multiply for unknown reasons. Such tumors can exist in the body for twenty years or more and cause no harm. More frequently, however, cell division is much more rapid, and the cells spread to encircle surrounding tissues. Some cells may invade the blood or LYMPHATIC SYSTEM and spread throughout the body. These cells may lodge in the BRAIN, LIVER, LUNGS, or bone marrow and divide to produce more tumors. Such growths must be completely destroyed as soon as discovered. Methods used are surgery, X-rays, chemicals, burning, hormones, freezing, and LASER.

Benign tumors are growths which produce SYMPTOMS because of their size and position in the body. A large tumor of the THYROID gland is a goiter. A tumor of the PANCREAS may produce excessive INSULIN. Tumors may press on nerves and cause pain or paralysis.

The cause of tumor growth is not entirely understood. We know excessive hormones and certain chemicals can cause tumors. Excessive sun (ultraviolet light) can produce skin cancer. Failure of the body's immune system may allow a small tumor to "escape" and spread rapidly throughout the body.
                                              B. M. H.

SEE ALSO: CANCER

Tuna

Tuna belong to the same family as the MACKEREL. They have cigar-shaped bodies that become very narrow at the point where the large lobed tail begins. Behind the *anal fin* and the second *dorsal fin* is a series of tiny finlets. In some species, scales are

Bluefin tuna is the largest of the bony fish

limited to a small area under the *pectoral fins.* Just before the *tail fin,* on the sides of the body, are three keels. The center one is large. Mackerel have only two.

The largest tuna is the *giant bluefin.* It may weigh 1,800 pounds (815 kilograms) and be 14 feet (4.3 meters) long. Usually, tuna weigh 60 to 300 pounds (27 to 136 kilograms). *Albacore* is a small (40 pound or 18 kilogram) bluefin tuna with a very long pectoral fin. Its white meat furnishes the best grade of canned tuna. *Bonitos* are tuna with stripes on the upper body. Species of *yellow-fin* tuna live in warm waters.   J.C.K.

Tundra (TUHN-druh) Tundra, the coldest BIOME, is a belt of ground around the northernmost part of North America, Europe, and Asia. The frozen plain is bare and rocky. The atmosphere is thin, and there is little precipitation. The growing season is short. The ground is low in nutrients and is constantly heaving from freezing and thawing.

Tundra can be divided into the arctic and the alpine. The latter is farther south of the pole in mountain areas. Permafrost may be 2,000 feet (609.6 meters) thick. Temperatures range from 50° to -60° F. (10° to -51° C.). In summer the ground thaws only a few centimeters to less than a meter.

Animal life in the tundra fluctuates with the food supply. The BIOMASS is low since decomposers function during the short summer. Plant life includes lichen, moss, sedge, lupine, heath, and bearberry. Short trees and shrubs grow in the south alpine tundra. Most plants reproduce by runners or root propagation rather than seeds.

Animals include musk ox, caribou, elk, wolf, lemming, polar bear, snow goose, and arctic hare. In the cold waters are fish, whales, seals, and walruses. There are no reptiles and only one species of amphibian, the wood frog. Animals must migrate or remain active all year. They cannot hibernate in the frozen ground.

The natural resources are coal, oil, iron, nickel, gold, and uranium. The tundra is another delicate ecosystem that man is moving into, and it needs protection.   H.J.C.

Courtesy Society For Visual Education, Inc.

In the northernmost regions of the tundra, the ground remains frozen most of the year

Tungsten (TUHNG-stuhn) Tungsten is a rare, gray-white metal that belongs to the CHROMIUM family of elements. Because it is hard and resists corrosion, it is used in making the finest cutting tools. It is used for filaments in electric light bulbs because it has a high melting point.

Tungsten has symbol W from its old name, *wolfram.* Its atomic number is 74 and its atomic weight is 183.85.

Tungsten is never found alone in nature. It is found in combination with calcium in the mineral *scheelite* and in combination with iron and manganese in the mineral *wolframite.* These minerals are all salts of the oxide of tungsten and when heated with carbon will give metallic tungsten.

China, with its rich supply of the brown-black wolframite, produces the most tungsten. The United States relies upon the gray or yellow mineral scheelite for its source of the metal. Scheelite and wolframite were once thought to be ores of tin, but in 1781 tungsten was recognized as an element.

"Tungsten" means "heavy stone," a term which refers to its high specific gravity of 19.3 grams per cubic centimeter.   J. M. C.
SEE ALSO: ELEMENTS, METAL

Tunicate see Chordata

Tuning fork see Overtones, Sound

Turbellaria see Planaria

Turbine (TER-bihn) A turbine is a machine which changes the energy of a moving liquid, or gas, into a form of energy which will do work. A turbine is usually named according to the force which drives it. Water turbines, steam turbines, and gas turbines are the three main types.

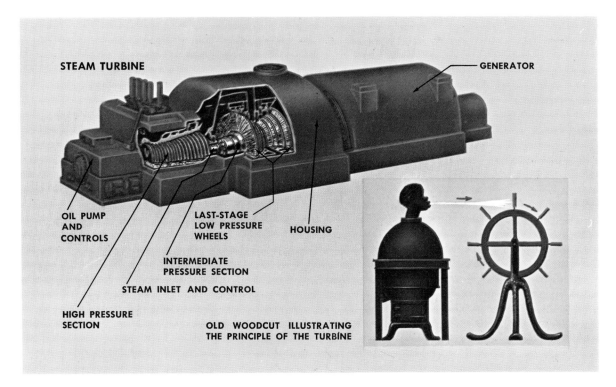

STEAM TURBINE

GENERATOR

OIL PUMP
AND
CONTROLS

LAST-STAGE
LOW PRESSURE
WHEELS

HOUSING

INTERMEDIATE
PRESSURE SECTION

STEAM INLET AND CONTROL

HIGH PRESSURE
SECTION

OLD WOODCUT ILLUSTRATING
THE PRINCIPLE OF THE TURBINE

Water wheels are among the oldest machines man has used to draw energy from nature to do his work. They were turned by a flowing river or stream with a shaft connected to provide simple rotary motion for milling and other uses.

The modern counterpart is the giant hydraulic turbine used at dams and waterfalls to produce electricity. This turbine wheel has many curved blades similar to those of a ship's propeller, and is mounted on a shaft which is connected to generators producing electricity. This turbine wheel is enclosed in a steel case with openings at the top and bottom, and is located at as low a level as possible completely under water beneath a dam or waterfall. The weight and force of a large flow of water rushing down through the turbine causes the blades to spin, turning the generator shaft at high speeds. This turbine, known as a *pressure* or *reaction* turbine, is very efficent.

Another type of water turbine, called a *pressureless* or *impulse* turbine, is used where there is a small amount of water falling from a great height. This wheel has many cup-shaped buckets around the outside diameter. It is driven by water from a nozzle striking the bucket blades, one at a time, at great speeds and force.

The *steam turbine* ranks as one of the most powerful types of machines that man has developed. The steam turbine is made up of a series of wheels which are mounted on a long shaft and increase in size from one end to the other. Each wheel is constructed with many blades, and rotates with the shaft between rows of fixed guide vanes attached to the turbine housing. The steam enters the housing with great pressure, and, directed against the smallest turbine wheel, causes it to rotate as the steam moves on to the next wheel. As the steam moves, its pressure decreases and its volume increases.

The *gas turbine* utilizes a stream of hot gases from a burning fuel to rotate a series of turbine wheels. This type of turbine has a rotating shaft with the turbine wheels at one end and a compressor at the other end. Between is a combustion chamber in which the fuel-air mixture is heated. Air is taken in at the front end of the gas turbine, and compressed into the combustion chamber where fuel is added. As the mixture is ignited, the hot, burning gases rush against the turbine wheels, causing them to rotate; and this, in turn, rotates the compressor. In this manner, heat ENERGY is changed into mechanical energy, and the rotating shaft may be coupled to the workload.   R. J. J.

SEE ALSO: COMPRESSOR, ELECTRICITY, ENGINE, GENERATOR, HYDROELECTRIC POWER, JET PROPULSION, PRESSURE

Turbojet see Engine, Jet propulsion

Turboprop see Jet propulsion

U. S. Department of Agriculture photo
Young tom turkeys being raised on an experimental farm in Kansas

Turkey These birds are in an American family consisting of two species, the *Yucatan turkey,* which man has never been able to domesticate, and the *wild turkey* of Mexico and North America. There are five subspecies of the wild turkey. The southern Mexican subspecies is the ancestor of all domestic turkeys. Turkeys are the largest game birds and the largest of the domestic FOWL bred for meat.

The southern Mexican turkey was introduced into Europe in 1530 and later brought by the colonists to eastern North America. After the birds were introduced into Europe, they spread to the Near East. Thus it happened that an American bird was reintroduced into America with a name probably acquired in the country Turkey.

Turkeys spend most of their time on the ground. They have heavy bodies and short legs. Domestic turkeys have short wings, but a wild turkey might have a wingspread of almost 40 inches (101.6 centimeters). They have powerful legs, big feet, long necks covered with warty skin, and small, bald heads. The growth of skin that hangs down from the front of the head and laps across the beak is called a *leader* or *dewlap.* The fleshy red lobe on the neck is the *wattle.*

Though some varieties of domestic turkeys are white, most have vari-colored feathers—brown, red, green and black. The feathers shine with a metallic iridescence.

At mating time; the male, or *tom,* struts and gobbles and displays its array of tail feathers spread into a fan.

Turkeys eat seeds, acorns and insects. Young ones are vulnerable to a disease organism that is harbored in damp ground. C. L. K.

Turmeric (TER-mer-ick) Turmeric is an HERB grown for its useful roots. When dried and powdered, they make a yellow dye and a sharp spice for flavoring. This tropical perennial belongs to the *ginger* family and is native to China, India and the East Indies.

The large leaves and petioles are attached to a short stem. The light-yellow blooms are inflorescences of many small flowers. Processed turmeric is a chemical indicator, used for testing acidity and alkalinity. Its yellow color is used in butter. Its bitter taste is added to curry powder and other products needing some bitterness. H.J.C.

Turmeric

Turnip The part of the turnip plant that is eaten is really both root and stem. Leaves grow from the upper part and roots from the lower. In the first year, the turnip stores up food materials. The next year a yellow flower appears and the plant dies.

This biennial is grown in cool temperate areas and matures in about 70 days. The flavor becomes strong if the weather is too warm. The white to yellow root should be dug up before frost when it is no more than 3 inches (7.6 centimeters) in diameter. Older turnips become woody and are used for animal feed. The tops are used for greens. H.J.C.

Turnip

Turpentine Crude turpentine is obtained from a RESIN which a variety of pine trees produce. Crude turpentine is distilled from the resin and a purer product known as *oil of turpentine* is collected. This oil of turpentine is commonly called turpentine.

Turpentine is a colorless liquid which has a characteristic odor. Upon aging and exposure to air, this odor becomes even more pronounced. Since turpentine is an oil, it is insoluble in water; but as other oils, it is soluble in organic solvents such as benzene and ether. In industry, turpentine is used in paints and varnishes to allow them to penetrate wooden surfaces better. Turpentine is a fair solvent for rubber, sulfur, and iodine.

The word "turpentine" is derived from *terpene* which refers to a series of complex HYDROCARBONS. Turpentine is a mixture of some of these terpenes. The chemical formula for turpentine is $C_{10}H_{16}$.　　　M. S.

Turquoise (TUR-koyz) The best samples of turquoise mineral have a deep, greenish-blue color. It is noncrystalline and has a waxy luster when polished. In America, turquoise was first mined by the Southwest Indians in New Mexico and Arizona. These people still shape and mount them in silver to make prized ornaments.

The word turquoise is from the French word *Turkish* meaning stone. The first gems were brought into Europe by traders who got them in Persia, where they are still mined.

Geologically, turquoise is formed in the earth by deposits from ground-water solutions. It is a hydrous phosphate of copper and aluminum, formula

$$CuAl_6(PO_4)_4(OH)_8 \cdot 4H_2O.$$

It has a hardness of 5 to 6.　　　D. A. B.

Buchsbaum

The sea turtle's legs are flippers

Turtle A turtle is a reptile that crawls on short legs. Turtles have an attached shell-like house to cover and protect them. Some turtles live only in water, and others live only on land. Some turtles are capable of living both places.

Turtles, tortoises, and terrapins are all turtles; although the name *tortoise* is usually given to a land turtle. A turtle served as food is often called *terrapin.*

A turtle's shell is formed by the backbone and ribs growing together, then becoming covered with plate-like scales. The top shell, or *carapace,* is arched, making it stronger than a flat surface. The bottom shell, or *plastron,* is flat so that the turtle's legs can reach the ground. Some turtles have leathery shells, or shells that cover part of the body. A frightened turtle pulls its head, legs and tail into its shell where its neck folds up like the letter S.

A painted turtle sun-bathing on a log
Courtesy Society For Visual Education, Inc.

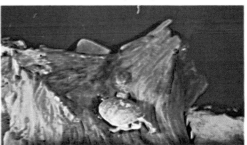

Spiderweb turquoise from New Mexico
J. Daniel Willems

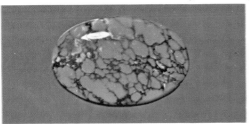

1—Common spotted turtle
2—Giant tortoise
3—South American land turtle
4—Diamondback terrapin
5—Warm water green turtle
6—Common snapping turtle
7—Box turtle
8—Australian snake-necked turtle

All pictures Courtesy Society For Visual Education, Inc.

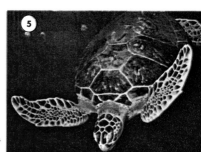

Turtles have no teeth, but they have horny beaks that can bite hard. The common snapping turtle of North America may grow to 2 feet (.6 meter) in length. It can snap angrily in all directions, even over its back. A mishandled snapper will take off a finger with one quick chop of its beak.

Turtles hatch from eggs. The female digs a hole with its hind feet in soft dirt or sand, or in a rotting log. It lays the eggs in the hole, covers them with earth, and leaves them for the sun's warmth to hatch. It never sees the baby turtles. When the turtles hatch they crawl toward water for protection from animals, for their shells are still soft. Most types of young turtles eat tadpoles, snails, worms, and insects. Each summer the turtle's shell adds an edge to its carapace plates, marking another year's age. Old turtles may have their plate borders worn away. Some species of turtles live longer than any other backboned animal. Some have lived over one hundred years.

Turtles are cold-blooded. They must hibernate in the winter. There have been turtles for 175,000,000 years. Some sea turtles have grown to be 12 feet (3.7 meters) long. The Galapagos turtle of today may weigh 500 pounds (225 kilograms).

The brown and yellow tortoise shell comes from the hawk's-bill turtle. Mud turtles, also known as musk turtles or stinkpots because of their odor, will seize a fisherman's bait. They have a vicious bite. The box turtle, dark brown with yellow spots, is relatively harmless. It destroys garden insects and also likes soft or cooked vegetables. P. G. B.

SEE ALSO: REPTILIA

Turtledove see Dove

Tusks Tusks are changed, or modified, front teeth. They are found on several kinds of animals, such as the elephant, walrus, and hippopotamus. Animals use their tusks to defend themselves. Some animals have become endangered because people kill them for the IVORY that comes from their tusks.

In man, the four front TEETH (upper or lower) are called *incisors.* Elephant tusks are long, thickened upper incisors. They lack the enamel coat of human and some other mammalian teeth. Under the enamel layer, the human tooth is composed of dentine. The elephant tusk is a very hard dentine, commonly called ivory.

Tusks of the wild boar (PIG family), hippopotamus, and walrus are modified canine teeth. These animals use their tusks as weapons. The walrus also uses them to pull itself up onto ice and to get clams and other food from the sea bottom.   H.J.C.

Tweeter see High fidelity

Twilight Twilight is daylight which occurs after sunset or just before dawn. It is caused by the reflection of sunlight from the upper parts of the atmosphere while the sun is as much as 18° below the horizon.

Twilight sleep Twilight sleep was a kind of ANESTHESIA used for women in childbirth. It is rarely used today because it caused patients to scream and thrash, even though memory of such behavior was blocked.

Twins see Multiple births

Tympanic membrane see Ear

Tyndall effect (TINN-duhl) When a person looks at the sunlit sky, he sees a blue color. When he looks at some kinds of smoky air under white light, the smoke appears bluish to brownish. The changed color of such lighted objects results from a scattering effect of tiny particles in the air. This is called the Tyndall effect. The same effect makes sunlight appear golden at sunrise and sunset.
SEE: COLLOIDAL SUSPENSION, LIGHT

Type see Printing

Some animals, past and present, that have tusks

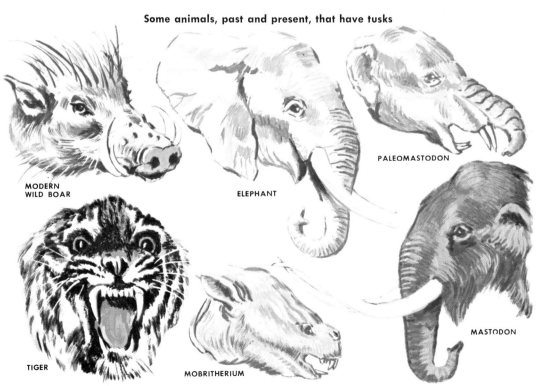

MODERN WILD BOAR

ELEPHANT

PALEOMASTODON

TIGER

MOBRITHERIUM

MASTODON

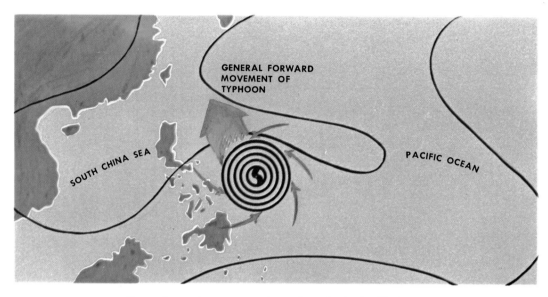

Formation and movement of a typhoon in the Pacific Ocean

Typhoid fever (TIE-foyd) Typhoid fever is a disease that affects the intestines. It is spread by foods that contain the germs. In times of disaster, such as flood, fire, or war, sewers frequently break and contaminate drinking water. At such time, typhoid can become EPIDEMIC.

Typhoid was described as early as 400 B.C. It is caused by BACTERIA (*Salmonella typhose*). The bacteria are excreted in the urine and feces of infected persons. If sewage becomes mixed with a water supply, an entire city can be infected. Unclean hands can contaminate foods. People who recover from typhoid may become CARRIERS and excrete the bacteria for years. Such people are forbidden to handle food in this country. Typhoid has been practically eliminated in the United States by sanitation, sewage disposal, and food inspection procedures.

Typhoid causes a fever which may last a month. It can cause ulcers in the intestine that may hemorrhage or perforate, causing PERITONITIS. Vaccination may prevent the disease or lessen its severity.

Paratyphoid fever is a related but milder disease. TYPHUS is a different disease. B. M. H.
SEE ALSO: DISEASE, TYPHUS FEVER

Typhoon (ty-FOON) A typhoon is a tropical cyclone of low pressure air. It creates violent storms. Tropical cyclones are found in many areas of the world. Even though different names are given to the storm, they are identical. A typhoon occurs in the western Pacific Ocean. In the West Indies, the same type of storm is called a *hurricane*.

Typhoons generate very high winds of 75 miles (120 kilometers) or more per hour. They also bring heavy rains and exceptionally high tides to land areas that they hit. Typhoons derive their energy largely from the heat that is given off in the condensation of some of the great amount of moisture in tropical air. Typhoons of the Northern Hemisphere move in a general northwesterly direction. H.S.G.
SEE ALSO: HURRICANE

Typhus fever (TYE-fuhs) This deadly and highly contagious disease is caused by a microscopic organism (*rickettsia*) that enters the body through the bite of the body LOUSE or rat FLEA. In about ten days, a sudden fever, headache, and delirium occur. A VACCINE is used for prevention.

Typhus spreads rapidly when people are crowded together in dirty surroundings with poor food and ventilation. It has been called by such names as "jail fever," "ship fever," and "war camp fever." To prevent an EPIDEMIC, rats must be eliminated and clothing sprayed with insecticide. B. M. H.

Typography see Printing

Tyrannosaurus see Dinosaur

Ulcer An ulcer is an open sore that may develop from an infected scratch or break in the skin. These sores are usually round and filled with a yellow crust of PUS. More often, however, ulcers occur in the stomach or intestine. These are called *peptic ulcers.*

Peptic ulcers result from erosion of the cells of the stomach and upper intestine (*duodenum*). When the body is healthy, a coating of mucous protects the cells from the digestive action of HYDROCHLORIC ACID and ENZYMES secreted by the stomach. Emotional or physical strain can cause blood vessels to contract, which in turn impairs nutrition to the cells. Acid and the digestive enzymes can then act on the lining of the stomach or intestine and produce an ulcer. The ulcer may burrow through the stomach wall (perforate) and cause PERITONITIS. It may erode a blood vessel and cause severe hemorrhage.

Ulcer pain occurs when the stomach is empty; it can be relieved by milk or antacids. The drug Cimetidine prevents release of acid by the stomach and is also useful in attempting to heal an ulcer. If complications occur, surgery may be necessary, either to remove acid-secreting areas of the stomach or to cut the stimulating nerves so the ulcer will heal. B.M.H./E.S.S.

Ulna see Skeleton

Ultraviolet ray see Ray, ultraviolet

Umbilical cord see Embryology

Umbra The umbra is the darkest portion of a shadow, whereas the PENUMBRA is lighter. The former term is mainly used for describing an ECLIPSE of the sun or the moon.

During a total eclipse of the sun, an observer in the umbra portion of the moon's shadow will see complete coverage of the sun by the moon. Those who observe from the penumbra portion of the shadow will see only a partial covering of the sun by the moon. Astronomers also use "umbra" to describe the darkest portion of a *sunspot,* which in this case represents an area of the sunspot that is cooler than the surrounding penumbra (hotter) area. P.P.S.
SEE ALSO: SUNSPOTS

Undulant fever see Animal diseases

Ungulata The word means "hoofed." At one time it was the name for an order of mammals. Today they are put into two new orders, called Perissodactyla and ARTIODACTYLA.

The perissodactylas are odd-toed animals such as the horse, tapir, and rhinoceros. None of the living ones are native to the United States, but fossil remains of this group have been found in this country.

The artiodactylas are even-toed animals such as the cow, camel, giraffe, and hippopotamus. They are the most abundant and successful, and the latter are two of the big-game herds of Africa. Their numbers are dwindling as the hunters and poachers move in.

Present-day ungulates walk on fewer toes and have a larger body size and higher intelligence than their ancestors. The herbivorous ungulates have incisors for cutting and molars for grinding, and often the canines are missing. H.J.C.

Unicellular organism see Protozoa

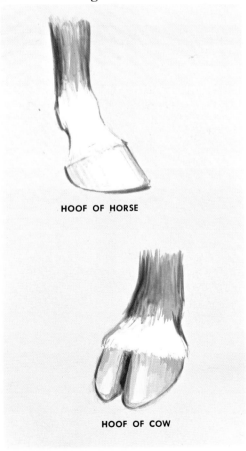

HOOF OF HORSE

HOOF OF COW

Unidentified flying object (UFO) An

unidentified flying object is a term commonly used to describe an object that appears to be flying in the sky but cannot be readily identified by the observer. Often UFOs appear as fast-moving spots of light and are called *flying saucers*. Although most UFOs can be explained, many people believe them to be spacecraft from other planets.

Thousands of UFO sightings have been reported in over seventy countries. Some are described as mysterious light sources, others seem to be solid cigar or saucer shapes that emit lights and sound. Two common characteristics of a UFO seem to be rapid acceleration to great speeds and remarkable maneuverability.

Strange objects in the sky have been recorded for nearly 2,000 years. Current public interest was aroused in 1947 when a U.S. private pilot vividly described a string of UFOs near Mt. Rainier. He was the first to call them "flying saucers." Among the many sightings since then, large numbers have been reported by reliable observers.

The U.S. Air Force established *Operation Blue Book* in 1948 to investigate all reports. The investigating team was able to explain most UFO sightings as aircraft, weather balloons, meteors, atmospheric phenomena (such as temperature inversions), and other identifiable sources. Many UFO reports came from people who sighted the planet Venus under certain conditions (just before sunrise or after sunset). It must be noted that about 10 percent of the sightings are without acceptable explanations. These reports require careful analysis to determine the credibility and reliability of the observers.

Operaton Blue Book is no longer active. However, many people in many different nations continue to investigate UFOs.

Although many scientists are skeptical about UFOs, the possibility that some natural but unknown phenomena exist cannot be ignored. Perhaps there is also a possibility that UFOs are the vehicles of intelligent life from other solar systems.

R.J.J

Universe The universe includes all

the members of the solar system, all the stars in the Milky Way, all of the other stars and galaxies in space, and the space between them. Man does not know where the universe ends—or whether it ends at all. Since ancient times men have been pushing back the boundaries of the known universe. They have wondered, and still wonder, how the universe began and how it will end, when it began, and if it will end.

In ancient times men thought that Earth was the center of the universe. They thought the earth was flat and had a dome fitting down on top of it. The dome was dotted with tiny lights—the STARS. They thought the sun and the stars and the moon were pulled across the dome every day. The Greeks altered this theory. They, too, thought that Earth was the center of the universe, but they imagined that a series of spheres surrounded the earth. These spheres held the sun, the moon, the planets, and the stars. They all revolved around Earth. COPERNICUS and GALILEO introduced, and tried to prove, the theory that the sun, not Earth, was the center of the universe. This idea was difficult for men to accept. Today it is known that neither Earth, nor the sun, nor even the Milky Way galaxy, is the center of the universe. If a person could look at the whole known universe, he would probably notice the MILKY WAY galaxy. But he might not even single out the sun, much less one of the small planets that revolve around it—earth. So far is the earth from being the

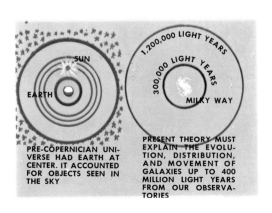

PRE-COPERNICIAN UNIVERSE HAD EARTH AT CENTER. IT ACCOUNTED FOR OBJECTS SEEN IN THE SKY

PRESENT THEORY MUST EXPLAIN THE EVOLUTION, DISTRIBUTION, AND MOVEMENT OF GALAXIES UP TO 400 MILLION LIGHT YEARS FROM OUR OBSERVATORIES

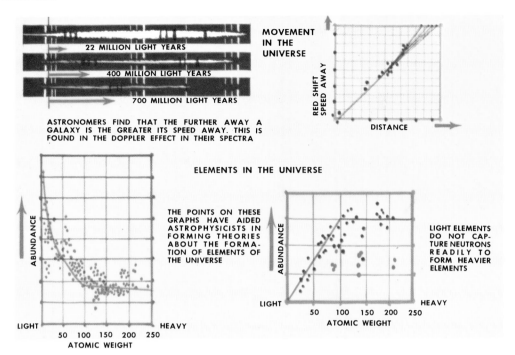

22 MILLION LIGHT YEARS

400 MILLION LIGHT YEARS

700 MILLION LIGHT YEARS

ASTRONOMERS FIND THAT THE FURTHER AWAY A GALAXY IS THE GREATER ITS SPEED AWAY. THIS IS FOUND IN THE DOPPLER EFFECT IN THEIR SPECTRA

MOVEMENT IN THE UNIVERSE

RED SHIFT SPEED AWAY

DISTANCE

ELEMENTS IN THE UNIVERSE

THE POINTS ON THESE GRAPHS HAVE AIDED ASTROPHYSICISTS IN FORMING THEORIES ABOUT THE FORMATION OF ELEMENTS OF THE UNIVERSE

ABUNDANCE

LIGHT   HEAVY

50   100   150   200   250

ATOMIC WEIGHT

ABUNDANCE

LIGHT   HEAVY

50   100   150   200   250

ATOMIC WEIGHT

LIGHT ELEMENTS DO NOT CAPTURE NEUTRONS READILY TO FORM HEAVIER ELEMENTS

center of the universe that, compared to the entire known universe, Earth would be less significant than a guppy swimming in the Pacific Ocean.

Many people might like to think that the universe has always been just as it is today and that it will always remain the same. But astronomers know that the universe changes. Stars die out. New stars are formed. Stars move in space. Galaxies move. Astronomers use the information they have about the known objects in space—their composition, their directions and speeds, their changes in appearance—to theorize about the origin, evolution, and future of all the rest of the universe.

Most astronomers today agree that observations of distant galaxies indicate that the entire universe is steadily expanding. Since all the galaxies are moving away from each other, astrophysicists sometimes imagine that the universe is an enormous sphere that is expanding like a soap bubble or a balloon that is being blown up.

The recent advancements in the science of NUCLEAR SCIENCE enable astronomers to present new theories about the origin of the universe. The study of nuclear reactions leads to the study of chemical elements, how they are formed, and why they occur in the proportions that they do. When astronomers put such data together with data collected by astrophysicists, they can piece together a little more of the puzzle. The astrophysicists can study what elements are in outer space and in what proportions they occur there. They know that there is a predominance of hydrogen in stars and space. There is also a large amount of helium. Hydrogen and helium are the simplest and lightest elements. High temperature and high pressure are necessary to start the nuclear reactions to form elements.

Some astrophysicists theorize that about 13 million years ago, all the matter in the universe was packed into a tight, small ball—a *primeval nucleus.* This nucleus exploded and began to expand. In the early stages of expansion, the stars and the galaxies were formed. As the universe continues to expand, the galaxies will move at increasing speeds and will continue to recede from each other forever. The density of the galaxies in the universe is forever decreasing. In some far distant epoch, the only stars visible from the earth, if it still existed, would be those of man's own galaxy. This theory is one form of the *evolutionary theory* of the universe and is so called because it assumes that the universe began at a finite time. It depends upon Einstein's theory of general RELATIVITY.

Another form of the evolutionary theory also states that after the explosion of the

SOLAR SYSTEM

primeval nucleus the stars and galaxies were formed. As the universe expanded, the rate of expansion slowed down. Eventually the forces of mutual gravitational attraction between the galaxies will overcome the expansion. The universe will then start to contract. Eventually all matter will have again contracted into a primeval nucleus. After eons the primeval nucleus will again explode, and expansion will start again. This is the *pulsating model* of the evolutionary theory. Since all matter would be destroyed in this contraction and expansion, astronomers can, of course, have no direct way of determining whether this is a true model.

The *steady-state* theory states that the universe had no beginning and will have no end. Instead of an explosion of a primeval nucleus in the far, far distant past, astronomers who support the steady-state theory claim that matter is being created all the time, at an exceedingly slow rate, in the space between the galaxies. This new matter is hydrogen, and it will eventually form clusters of galaxies. Each new cluster forms, expands, ages, and dies, but other new clusters are always forming so the universe will always have the same density and there will always be galaxies of all ages in the universe. Thus the universe is always the same in any epoch. A major trouble with the steady-state theory is that it violates the laws of THERMODYNAMICS.

The evolutionary theory, on the other hand, states that all galaxies are the same age. The difference in age is apparent, since the light from the most distant galaxies left them many billions of years ago when they were younger.   C. L. K.

SEE ALSO: SPACE, SUN

Ural Mountains see Asia

Uranium (yoo-RAY-nee-um) In 1896 a French chemist, Henri Becquerel, happened to put a piece of mineral containing uranium near a covered photographic plate. He was surprised when he found that the plate was fogged as if it had been exposed to light. After experimenting, he found that some kind of invisible ray came from the uranium. This phenomenon is known today as *radioactivity*.

The mineral Becquerel put near the plate was PITCHBLENDE. In 1898, PIERRE AND MARIE CURIE tried to isolate the radioactive material from a ton of pitchblende. They discovered that pitchblende itself was more radioactive than pure uranium. The first radioactive substance they isolated from pitchblende was called *polonium,* named after Madame Curie's native country, Poland. Later she isolated a small amount of RADIUM. Experiments conducted later by other scientists led to the discovery of other radioactive elements.

Uranium is found chiefly in uraninite. In pitchblende, 80 percent is in the form of an oxide, U_3O_8. *Carnotite* also contains uranium, VANADIUM, and POTASSIUM.

Uranium is not considered a rare element. It is found in moderate quantities in Canada, the Republic of the Congo, Czechoslovakia, Colorado, and Utah. Uranium is a metal that

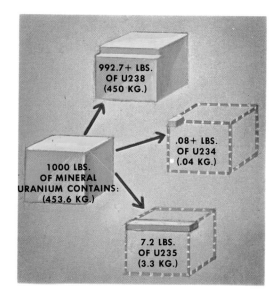

1000 LBS. OF MINERAL URANIUM CONTAINS: (453.6 KG.)

992.7+ LBS. OF U238 (450 KG.)

.08+ LBS. OF U234 (.04 KG.)

7.2 LBS. OF U235 (3.3 KG.)

is silvery, about as dense as tungsten, slightly softer than steel, and the heaviest element that occurs in any abundance. Its atomic number is 92 and its atomic weight is 238.03. It has several isotopes, some of which are used in man's nuclear fission reactions and NUCLEAR REACTORS. Its oxidation numbers (valences) are $+3$, $+4$, $+5$, and $+6$.

Uranium, like all other radioactive substances, goes through radioactive disintegration, emitting three different kinds of radiations—alpha, α; beta, β; and gamma, γ, rays. The half-life of U^{238} is 4.5 x 10^9, or 4½ billion years.

E.Y.K.

SEE ALSO: NUCLEAR ENERGY, NUCLEAR GLOSSARY. NUCLEAR SCIENCE, NUCLEAR REACTORS

Uranus (YOOR-uh-nuhs) Uranus is one of the four *gas giant* planets that revolve around the sun. It is the seventh planet away from the sun. Its path is between the paths of SATURN and NEPTUNE. Uranus and Neptune look very much alike through telescopes. They are about the same size, and have a greenish color. These two planets are sometimes called twins.

Uranus speeds up in its journey around the sun when it approaches Neptune. After it passes Neptune, Uranus slows down. Neptune's gravity causes the changes in Uranus' speed. From studying these changes in the speed of Uranus astronomers discovered Neptune. Still the position of Uranus did not fit the tables astronomers had charted for it. Eventually PLUTO, the farthest known planet, was also discovered from the study of Uranus' orbit, since Pluto influences Uranus' orbit, too.

Uranus was discovered in 1781 by William Herschel, an amateur astronomer. When he first observed this heavenly body, Herschel thought it was a comet. He noticed, though, that its path was circular, like that of a planet. It did not have a tail, as comets do. Thus Herschel decided that it must be a planet.

Uranus can be seen without a telescope, but one needs to know exactly where to look for it. It looks like a very faint star.

With a telescope, Uranus looks like a small green disk. Its greatest difference

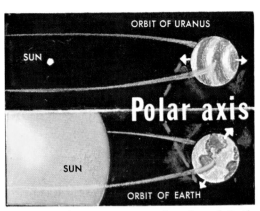

The orbit of Uranus compared to that of Earth

from the other planets is that it is tilted much more than the others. Sometimes one of Uranus' poles points almost directly at Earth. Then this planet seems to roll around the sun like a ball instead of spinning around the sun like a top.

Uranus rotates in 17 hours and 14 minutes, but because of its extreme angle of inclination (98 degrees) the days and nights—or seasons—are very long. When the sun rises at the north pole of the planet, day lasts for 42 years. When the sun sets, night lasts for 42 years also. Even during the long light period, however, Uranus is not warm. Its temperature is less than $-300°$ F ($-184°$ C). Uranus is too far from the sun to receive much heat or light from it. The sun is about 1,785,000,000 miles (2.87 billion kilometers) from Uranus. Consequently, days on the planet Uranus are cold and dim.

Uranus's orbit is nearly circular. It takes about 84 earth-years for this planet to get around the sun. It travels about 15,000 miles (24,000 kilometers) per hour. Uranus has a diameter of about 32,000 miles (51,499 kilometers).

Until the *Voyager 2* space probe visited the outer Solar System, astronomers could not be certain about the properties of distant planets. The great distances involved made observations with earth-bound telescopes difficult. *Voyager 2* reached Uranus in 1985 and radioed data back to Earth. Uranus's atmosphere was found to be about 5,000 miles (8,000 kilometers) deep. It consists of 99% hydrogen and helium. High in the atmosphere is a layer of thin methane-ice clouds, much like the clouds of Neptune.

The surface of the planet is liquid. Scientists think that the planet has a core of molten rock about the size of Earth. Astronomers do not believe that there could be life similar to ours on Uranus because of the extreme cold in the planet's outer layers. A thin *corona*, or halo, of hydrogen surrounds the planet. Sunlight falling on the corona causes it to radiate light in the ultraviolet part of the spectrum. Scientists call this radiation *electroglow*.

In early 1977 a group of astronomers using earth-based instruments made a startling discovery about Uranus. They found evidence, during the *occultation* (eclipse) of a bright star by Uranus, that a series of rings circles the planet. *Voyager 2* reported that the planet has a complex ring system. There are 10 narrow rings composed of dark particles and one broad, thin ring. There may be over 100 ringlets of tiny particles. Although the ring system of Uranus is similar to that of Saturn, Uranus's rings are not as large as Saturn's and are much closer to the planet.

Uranus has 5 major moons and 10 small moons. The small moons were discovered by *Voyager 2.* The moons' orbits around Uranus's equator and the changes in the angle of the equator cause the moons to have strange motions when viewed from Earth.

The surfaces of the moons are covered with craters and fractures. The largest moons, Titania and Oberon, are very much alike in size and appearance. Oberon has a mountain about 12 miles (19 kilometers) high. All the moons appear to be in synchronous rotation. This means that they keep the same side facing Uranus as they orbit the planet.   C.L.K.

SEE ALSO: NEPTUNE, PLUTO, SATELLITE, SOLAR SYSTEM

Urea (yoo-REE-uh) Urea is the commonest waste material in human urine. All nitrogen from excess protein in man and other mammals is changed, first to ammonia, and then to less poisonous urea. From six to eighteen grams of urea collect, in solution, in the human urinary bladder during a twenty-four-hour period.

Rouelle identified urea in 1773. It was the first organic compound ever prepared in a laboratory. This synthesis was accomplished by WOEHLER in 1824. Urea can be broken down to ammonia and carbon dioxide by heat, or by the action of enzymes. The formula of urea is $CO(NH_2)_2$ and the molecular weight is 60.   M. S.

SEE ALSO: ORGANIC COMPOUNDS, PROTEIN

Ureter see Excretory system, Kidney

Urethra see Excretory system, Kidney

Dr. Harold Clayton Urey

Urey, Harold Clayton (1893-1981) Dr. Urey is an American chemist who was awarded the Nobel Prize for Chemistry (1934) for isolating heavy hydrogen. His research helped greatly in the production or uranium for the construction of the atomic bomb.

Harold Urey was born in Walkerton, Indiana, on April 29, 1893. Despite financial difficulties after his father's death, his mother sent him through the county grade schools and high school. After graduation, Urey taught for three years in rural schools. When his family moved to Montana, he followed, and attended the University of Montana.

After receiving his Ph.D. degree at the University of California in 1923, he went to Copenhagen as American - Scandinavian Foundation Fellow to study for a year under the great atomic physicist Niels Bohr.

As an associate professor at Columbia University he performed his first great experiments. In 1931, he discovered heavy hydrogen. He named his discovery *deuterium* from the Greek word meaning second place.

The value of heavy hydrogen to biologists has been enormous. By using it as a tracer element, they can now study proteins, while formerly they had been able to study only simple food-stuffs. They can also explore (with heavy hydrogen) the processes by which living creatures manufacture their own flesh out of the foods they eat.

By 1938 Dr. Urey had isolated heavy hydrogen and certain isotopes of oxygen, nitrogen, and carbon. These elements make up about 96 per cent of all food and flesh. Thus the new isotopes (particularly carbon-14) give research tools to many sciences.

In 1945 Dr. Urey left Columbia and joined the newly-formed Institute for Nuclear Studies at the University of Chicago. Upon retirement from the University of Chicago in 1958, he continued scientific work at the University of California.   D. H. J.

Uric acid (YOOR-ick) Uric acid is the primary end product of protein metabolism in reptiles and birds. In man and other mammals, urea is the common end product. Uric acid is present in small amounts in the urine of man and apes.

In crystalline form, uric acid is a white, odorless, tasteless, solid material. It is slightly soluble in water, but its true acidic nature is evident in its solubility in solutions of alkali hydroxides. Its molecular weight is 168.11; its chemical formula is $C_5H_4N_4O_3$. It is classified as a PURINE.   M. S.
SEE ALSO: ORGANIC COMPOUNDS, PROTEIN

Urine (YOOR-inn) Urine is an amber-colored liquid excreted by the kidneys. A pigment called *urochrome* gives it its color. The KIDNEYS filter waste materials from the blood. These wastes leave the body in the urine. An average adult excretes almost 3 pints (1.4 liters) of urine daily.

Urine is somewhat heavier than water. It contains compounds of sodium, chlorine, phosphorus, potassium, calcium, magnesium, and iron. It also contains urea, ammonia, uric acid and creatinine.

The examination of urine is very important in the detection of diseases.   G.A.D.
SEE ALSO: EXCRETORY SYSTEM

Ursa Major and Minor

Ursa Major and Minor (ER-suh) Ursa Major and Minor are two groups of stars that are supposed to represent bears in the sky. Ursa Major is the Larger Bear. Ursa Minor is the Smaller Bear. These constellations are probably not as famous as bears as they are for the other figures that some of their stars make—the *Big Dipper* and the *Little Dipper,* which revolve around POLARIS, first one and then the other being upside down.

These constellations can be seen on any clear night in the northern part of the world.

There are several interesting legends about the two star bears. Many early peoples recognized these formations as bears. Each nation made up its own legend. The North American Indians imagined the four bowl stars to be the bear. The three handle stars were hunters who chased the bear. The first hunter carried a bow and arrow. The second carried a pot for cooking the bear. The last one brought the fire. The hunters wounded the bear each autumn, the Indians thought, and as his blood dripped down on the forests it caused the leaves to redden.

In the Greek myths the Greater Bear was the beautiful Callisto, who was changed into a bear by Jupiter to protect her from the jealous Juno. Callisto's son, Arcas, was a hunter. One day he was about to kill the bear that was his mother. Jupiter intervened, changed Arcas into a bear, too.   C. L. K.
SEE ALSO: BIG AND LITTLE DIPPERS, CONSTELLATION

Uterus see Pregnancy

Uvula see Voice

Vaccine (VACK-seen) The term "vaccine" originally referred only to a substance containing the virus of cowpox. In the late 1700's, it was discovered by EDWARD JENNER that persons who had recovered from the disease cowpox could not get the more deadly disease, SMALLPOX. This was a great medical achievement. Jenner scratched the skin of well people and placed material taken from cowpox sores on the open scratch. He found that a man, in whom cowpox had been produced, was then unable to contract smallpox. This resistance against the disease is called *immunity*. *Vaccine* was the name Jenner gave to cowpox matter. The application of vaccine to the open scratch was called *vaccination*.

Today, the word *vaccine* refers to the modified bacteria or virus of any disease which is used to give protection to the person inoculated with it—without producing the severe infection that would result from the untreated virus. Most children in the United States have been immunized against smallpox as well as against diphtheria, tetanus and whooping cough (three in one vaccine). There are now vaccines to prevent many diseases. Some of these are typhoid, typhus, yellow fever, and influenza. Sometimes the word *vaccination* is used only in reference to smallpox. The application of other vaccines may then be called *inoculation*.

Bacteria can be grown on gelatin (*agar*). Viruses can be cultured by injecting them into chicken eggs. By successive transfers to new agar or chick eggs, the germs lose the ability to produce severe disease. They become weakened (*attenuated*), but they retain the ability to stimulate the system to produce ANTIBODIES against the disease. When the vaccine is inoculated into a person, the reaction is usually strong. An occasional "booster" will give lifelong protection.

Early in this century, two Frenchmen, Calmette and Guerin, cultivated and recultivated the bacillus that causes tuberculosis. It became attenuated and no longer produced TB in humans, yet it stimulated resistance to tuberculosis. This vaccine is called BCG after the bacillus and the originators. Another live, attenuated vaccine is the Sabin *oral* polio vaccine. Measles and mumps vaccines are given by injection. A virus may be the cause of some types of TUMORS, LEUKEMIA, and CANCER. If this proves to be true, a vaccine could be developed for treatment.

A second kind of vaccine is made from dead germs. It can be used only if the germs can be killed and still keep their chemical properties. This kind of vaccine is safe and, like the first type, causes blood to form antibodies. Instead of applying the vaccine to a scratch, it is injected with a hypodermic needle. The disadvantages of this type are that often the antibodies are not as numerous and do not last as long as the antibodies made with live germs. Many vaccines, including the *Salk poliomyelitis vaccine,* are of this killed-vaccine type.

In the third type, antibodies are produced as a result of injecting the treated poisons or *toxins* produced by a germ. Treatment has rendered these toxins harmless. Snakebite, tetanus, scarlet fever, and diphtheria are third type vaccines.

Passive immunity can be given to someone

Polio vaccine is produced by growing virus on monkey kidney tissue. The vaccine is stored for two months (left) while it is tested. Three different strains of virus growth are combined for the final vaccine, giving it greater effectiveness

Photos courtesy Chas. Pfizer & Co., Inc.

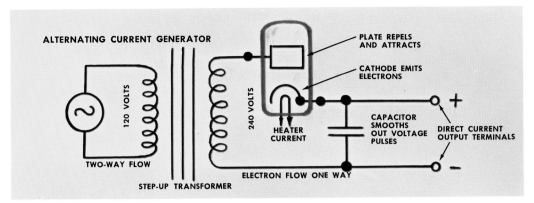

ALTERNATING CURRENT GENERATOR

PLATE REPELS AND ATTRACTS

CATHODE EMITS ELECTRONS

120 VOLTS

240 VOLTS

HEATER CURRENT

CAPACITOR SMOOTHS OUT VOLTAGE PULSES

DIRECT CURRENT OUTPUT TERMINALS

+

−

TWO-WAY FLOW

ELECTRON FLOW ONE WAY

STEP-UP TRANSFORMER

by injecting antibodies from a person who has successfully fought off the disease; for example, a new hyperimmune globulin protects people exposed to hepatitis B. Gamma globulin can also be given.

When a woman with the Rh negative blood factor has an Rh positive baby, some of the baby's blood cells escape at birth into the mother's bloodstream. This causes the mother to form antibodies which can negatively affect any future Rh positive babies. A simple shot of Rh positive antibodies (Rho Gam) at birth "fools" the mother's antibody-producing responses so that she can carry subsequent babies successfully.   J.C.K./E.S.S.

SEE ALSO: ANTIBODY; BACTERIOLOGY; DRUGS; SABIN, ALBERT; SALK, JONAS; VIRUS

Vacuole (VACK-yoo-ohl) A vacuole is a small round transparent-looking particle of fluid found in the cytoplasm of a cell. In protozoans, some vacuoles restore water balance and others digest food.

SEE: PROTOZOA

Vacuum (VACK-yoo-um) A vacuum is generally considered to be a totally empty space. A perfect vacuum is one which contains absolutely no molecules of gas. A perfect vacuum has not been made, though many vacuum tubes are almost free of molecules.

Partial vacuums are obtained in a closed container from which most of the gas molecules have been removed by means of an air pump. A perfect vacuum cannot be obtained because of the mechanical inefficiency of the air pumps. By employing a series of good vacuum pumps, a space can be evacuated to as little as 10^{-8} mm., or .00000001 mm., of mercury as compared to 760 mm. for atmospheric pressure.   A. E. L.

Vacuum tube A vacuum tube is the electronic control device used in radio-TV sets, scientific work, and industry. The vacuum tube is so important because it can amplify an electric current; that is, it can produce a strong electric current from a weak one.

Although thousands of different types of tubes are now in use, these are classified by the number of active electrical elements, or electrodes within them. *Diode* tubes, for instance, have two electrodes; *triodes,* three; *tetrodes,* four; and *pentodes,* five such electrodes. Diodes are used as *rectifiers,* or "electrical one-way streets." The others are used primarily to amplify electrical signals. Vacuum tubes may be seen in actual use when one looks in the back of most radio or TV sets.

As the name implies, all the active parts of the tube are contained within an envelope, a glass or metal tube from which air and other gases have been carefully removed. Each tube contains a CATHODE, a cylinder of nickel alloy coated with the oxides of barium and strontium. When brought to red heat by an internal electric heater, the cathode "boils-offs," or emits, billions of free electrons into the space around it.

In addition, the diode contains a second ELECTRODE, the plate, a cylinder of thin nickel alloy which surrounds the cathode. When the plate of the diode is made positive with respect to the cathode, the plate attracts the negative cathode-emitted electrons strongly, and a current then flows from cathode to the plate. But when the plate is negative, it repels the electrons, preventing their passage and effectively opening the circuit. Thus the diode serves as a rectifier and can convert alternating current into unidirectional current pulses. These may be smoothed by a capacitor into steady direct current.

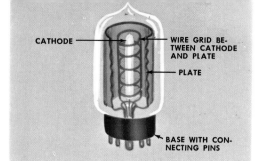

CATHODE —
WIRE GRID BE-
TWEEN CATHODE
AND PLATE

PLATE

BASE WITH CON-
NECTING PINS

The triode is made by placing a spiral, or network, of wires between the cathode and the plate. Being closer to the cathode than is the plate, this *grid* can exert a greater influence upon the emitted electrons. Normally the grid is operated at a slightly negative voltage with respect to the cathode, while the plate is made highly positive. The plate thus exerts a strong enough attractive force to overcome the partial repulsive effect of the negative grid.

When an alternating "signal" source is connected in series with the grid circuit, the signal first makes the grid more negative and then less negative. When the signal makes the grid more negative, the grid repels more of the electrons from the cathode and the current reaching the plate decreases. When the signal makes the grid less negative, the grid repels fewer electrons and the plate current increases. Thus a small change of voltage on the grid can cause a large change in the cathode-plate current, and amplification then results.

If sufficient amplification cannot be obtained with one tube, several may be connected in cascade, one after the other. Such an arrangement may increase the effects of a small voltage thousands of times.

If some of the output of an amplifier is fed back in proper phase into its input, or grid circuit, the circuit will act as an oscillator. An OSCILLATOR is an electronic alternating-current generator which generates currents having frequencies in the millions of cycles. Such oscillators are invaluable in radio, TV, long-distance telephony, and industrial processes.

Despite their usefulness, triodes are subject to difficulties due to electrical interaction between the grid and the plate. To eliminate this, a second grid, the *screen grid* is inserted between the first, or *control grid,* and the plate. The screen grid is kept at a potential somewhat less positive than the plate and thus acts as a shield, or screen, between the plate and control grid, preventing interaction between them. The screen-grid also improves the amplification properties of the tube. Such a tube, with a cathode, two grids, and a plate, is a tetrode.

The positive screen grid accelerates (speeds up) electrons traveling from the cathode to the plate. When these electrons reach the plate, they hit it with enough force to knock other electrons off. The secondary electrons knocked off the plate are attracted by the positive screen grid. If enough electrons are attracted to the grid, the plate current will decrease. In a pentode, an additional grid, the *suppressor,* is placed between the screen grid and the plate. The suppressor is usually internally connected to the cathode and is always at cathode potential. The suppressor effectively puts a neutral barrier between the secondary electrons and the screen grid and permits the electrons to return to the plate, thus increasing both stability and the amplification of the circuit.

A beam-power tube is a tetrode (or pentode) specially designed so that the electrons from the cathode travel in sheets between the wires of the screen grid to the plate. Beam-power tubes are frequently used as the final (power) tube in a radio or TV receiver. These tubes have a high power output and high efficiency.

All the tubes just described are primarily receiving tubes. The tubes used in radio, TV, and radar transmitters are similar, but larger so they can handle greater power. At microwave frequencies, special tubes must be used.

Tubes which depend for their operation on the nature of the gas with which they are filled are not, of course, vacuum tubes. Gas-filled tubes such as voltage regulator tubes and thyratrons are finding increasing use, particularly in industrial electronics. The term *electron tube* which covers both gas-filled and evacuated tubes is thus coming into general use, rather than vacuum tube.

Many of the jobs which tubes have done for years can also be done by transistors. For many applications, however, especially where subject to heat or radiation, tubes are still preferable and will be for many years.   C. F. R.

SEE ALSO: ELECTRICITY, ELECTRONICS, PHOTOELECTRICITY, RADIO, TELEVISION, TRANSISTOR

Vagus nerve see Nervous system

Valence (VAY-lens) In chemistry, valence is the ability of an element to combine with another element. Valence of an element is measured by the number of hydrogen atoms it can unite with or, if it will not unite with hydrogen, how many hydrogen atoms it will displace. Many ELEMENTS have more than one valence, and inert gases have zero valence.

Valley A valley is a depression, or channel, that is cut as running water or mountain glaciers move over the surface of the earth. A valley is usually V-shaped in its early stages of development, but the s des of the V may vary greatly in steepness. The rate at which a valley is cut depends upon the velocity of the running water and the type of *bedrock* through which the valley is being cut. When a glacier erodes a valley it gives it a characteristic U-shape rather than the V-shape of a river valley.

The V-shape of a river valley is caused by double *erosion.* The river deepens its valley by eroding its bed, but it also widens its valley by eroding its banks. River valleys do not retain the sharp V-shape forever. The deeper the river cuts into its valley, the closer it comes to the final or *base level.* As it cuts downward, it is also widening.

Any river or river system goes through three distinct stages as it develops over the years. These stages are youth, maturity, and old age. The speed at which a river goes through these stages varies greatly.　　H.S.G.

A glacial valley among mountains
Courtesy Society For Visual Education, Inc.

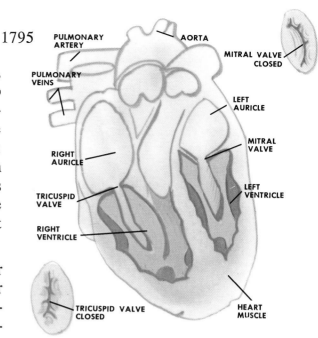

Valves, circulatory Valves are flaps of tissue extending out from the walls of the heart, medium-sized veins, and lymph vessels. They have a door-like action, preventing blood or lymph from flowing backward.

Two important valves in the mammalian HEART are the *mitral* and *tricuspid* valves located between the *auricles* and *ventricles.* In the center of each valve is a cartilage plate, covered on each side by elastic connective tissue containing smooth muscle.

Semilunar valves are crescent-shaped and found in the heart openings to the *pulmonary artery* and *aorta.* They are similar to the mitral and tricuspid valves.

Valves are commonly found in the veins coming back to the heart from the arms and legs. Usually they occur just before the junction or union of two branches. The free edges of the crescent-shaped valves face in the direction of the flow of blood. Beneath their covering of *endothelium,* in the cup part of the crescent, is elastic connective tissue. The CONNECTIVE TISSUE continues into the elastic membrane of the vein (*tunica intima*).

The construction of the valves in the lymph vessels is almost identical to those in the veins.　　J. C. K.

SEE ALSO: CIRCULATORY SYSTEM

Vampire see Bat

Van Allen belts see Atmosphere

Van de Graaff see Accelerator

Vanadium (vah-NAY-dee-uhm) Vanadium is element number 23. It is a metal, used in steel. Vanadium alloys are hard and malleable. It is found in several ores. It was first identified in 1830 by Nils Sefstrom, a Swedish chemist. It has chemical symbol V. Its atomic weight is 50.942.

It is very difficult to obtain pure vanadium because reduction from the ore requires very high temperatures. Also, pure vanadium reoxidizes very easily. Vanadium pentoxide (V_2O_5), one of the most widely used compounds, is used in the oxidation of napthalene and the manufacture of sulfuric acid. Other compounds are used in inks, paints and varnishes, insecticides, glass, etc. M. S.
SEE ALSO: ELEMENTS

Vane see Wind vane

Vanilla (vuh-NILL-uh) Vanilla is a vine related to the ORCHID. Man takes (extracts) a flavoring from it that is also called *vanilla*. The plant is tropical and has been cultivated in Mexico for a long time. It is grown widely in Madagascar and the Comoro and Reunion islands. A synthetic vanilla is often used today.

The vanilla plant is a climbing orchid

The vanilla vines climb by means of air rootlets which twine about trees. They live for ten years or more. A plant produces pods, or beans, 5 to 10 inches (12.7 to 25.4 centimeters) long, which resemble large green beans. They are picked when a yellow-green color, and allowed to dry and "cure." The inside pulp is an oily mass which contains small seeds. The beans are cut up, and by a complex process the vanilla flavoring is extracted from the pulp. Because the cost of production is high, substitutes (such as tonka beans) have been developed which are very good, although none are as good as true vanilla. D.J.I.

Vapor A vapor is the GAS form of a material which is usually a liquid. When water, for example, is heated, it becomes a vapor. The molecules of a vapor behave like those of an ordinary gas.
SEE: HUMIDITY, PRECIPITATION

Vapor lamp see Bulb, electric

Vapor pressure see Boyle's Law, Charles' Law, Gas

Vaporization see Evaporation, Heat of vaporization

Variable star see Star, variable

Varicose veins (VAIR-uh-kohss) These are VEINS that have become dilated from the pressure of the blood they contain. They appear as bluish, knotty tubes beneath the skin, most often in the legs. When valves in the veins no longer close, blood pools and forms clots. A clot can break off and travel to the lungs (EMBOLISM). Injection or surgical removal may be necessary. B. M. H.

Varnish Varnish is a clear coating to be sprayed or spread on a surface. It is made by dissolving resins in alcohol or volatile oils. A volatile oil is one from which vapor will escape rapidly, or dry quickly. It is made from a vegetable source.

Varnish made with alcohol as a drying agent is called *spirit varnish*. That made with volatile oil is an oil varnish. The resins used are secured from various trees; copal from Africa and lac, from which shellac is made, from Asia. No pigments (color) are added to varnish, as the chief use of varnish is to bring out the natural grain of wood and give it a protective finish.

Lacquer is somewhat similar in its content and drying qualities, and PIGMENT is added for color. A lacquer finish on wood gives a very smooth finish and is much thinner and harder than any paint coat. However, a lacquer coat is affected by steam heat and humidity, and will crack and chip from the wood. Lacquer is also used on metal when a delicate shading of color is needed in design.   P. G. B.

Vascular bundle (VASS-kyuh-ler)

Higher plants develop cells which form in groups during the first year of growth. These are called vascular bundles. They carry materials up and down the plant.

Vascular bundles have three kinds of tissues. *Xylem* conducts water and raw materials up the plant. *Phloem* carries food down to the roots. In woody plants, these two groups of cells are separated from each other by the vascular *cambium*. The cambium cells divide again and again, making more cells.

The vascular tissue produced after the first year, as in biennials and perennials, forms concentric circles rather than bundles. These are the ANNUAL RINGS. The primary xylem and phloem, or vascular bundle, gets pushed to the outside as new tissue is produced by the cambium.   H. J. C.

SEE ALSO: PLANT TISSUES

The structure of vascular bundles (in monocot and dicot plants)

Courtesy Society For Visual Education, Inc.

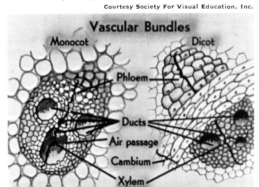

IF A FREE PARTICLE IS PUSHED UPWARD BY A FORCE OF 3 LBS. (13.3 NEWTONS) AT THE SAME TIME IT IS PUSHED RIGHT WITH A FORCE OF 4 LBS. (17.8 NEWTONS), THE VECTOR ANSWER FOR THE RESULT OF THESE TWO (VECTOR) FORCES IS SHOWN BY THE DIAGONAL VECTOR, 5 LBS. (22.2 NEWTONS).

Vector (VEHK-tehr)

When a quantity has both direction and magnitude (size), it is called a *vector* quantity. If the quantity has only magnitude, it is called a *scalar* quantity.

Such measurements as volume, mass, time, and temperature are usually thought of as merely numbers indicating a certain amount of each. These are some *scalar* quantities. On the other hand, when one thinks of displacement, velocity, and ACCELERATION, the idea of direction, as well as amount, comes to mind.

When the magnitude of the vector quantity is considered without regard for its direction, it becomes a scalar quantity. For instance, if one is interested only in the rate at which an automobile can travel regardless of direction, the VELOCITY becomes a scalar quantity designated as speed. Similarly, length may be the scalar quantity of the vector displacement.

In a diagram, a vector quantity is generally indicated by drawing an arrow pointed in the proper direction. The point of the arrow is called the *terminus,* and the butt end of the arrow is called the *origin.* In mathematical expressions, a vector quantity is designated by drawing a small arrow above the letter used to represent the quantity, such as A or B, or, more often, the A or B symbols will be printed in bold-face type, such as **A**.   A. E. L.

Conversion Factors to Metric Measurement

Length

1 inch = 25.4 millimeters (mm) exactly
1 inch = 2.54 centimeters (cm) exactly
1 foot = 0.3048 meters (m) exactly
1 yard = 0.9144 meters (m) exactly
1 mile = 1.609344 kilometers (km) exactly

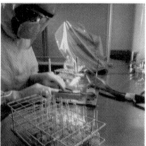

Area

1 square inch = 6.4516 square centimeters (cm^2) exactly
1 square foot = 0.092903 square meters (m^2)
1 square yard = 0.836127 square meters (m^2)
1 square acre = 0.404686 hectares (ha)
1 square mile = 2.58999 square kilometers (km^2)

Cubic Measure

1 cubic inch = 16.387064 cubic centimeters (cm^3) exactly
1 cubic foot = 0.0283168 cubic meters (m^3)
1 cubic yard = 0.764555 cubic meters (m^3)

US Liquid Measure

1 fluid ounce = 29.5735 milliliters (ml)
1 fluid ounce = 0.2957 deciliters (dl)
1 pint = 0.473176 liters (l)
1 gallon = 3.78541 liters (l)

US Dry Measure

1 pint = 0.550610 liters (l)
1 bushel = 35.2391 liters (l)

Weight

1 grain = 0.0647989 grams (g)
1 ounce = 28.3495 grams (g)
1 pound = 0.453592 kilograms (kg)
1 short ton = 0.907185 metric tons (t)
1 UK ton = 1.01605 metric tons (t)

Temperature

To convert Fahrenheit to Centigrade (Celsius) complete the following equation. $(F° - 32) \times 5 \div 9 = C°$